A New Pentecost

And there will be a new Pentecost! . . .

Pope John XXIII
December 8, 1963
Feast of the Immaculate
Conception

*For all things are yours . . . . whether the world,
or life, or death; or things present, or things
to come—all are yours, and you are Christ's
and Christ is God's.*

1 Cor. 3:22–23

We are charged to bring the future to birth!

Charles Péguy

A
New Pentecost

BY

Rev. James Fitzpatrick

B. HERDER BOOK CO.
ST. LOUIS & LONDON

IMPRIMATUR:
†Joseph Cardinal Ritter
Archbishop of St. Louis

December 31, 1965

GRATEFULLY DEDICATED
TO
MY FATHER AND MOTHER
JOHN AND MARY FITZPATRICK

Introduction

Behold, now is the acceptable time: behold,
now is the day of salvation!

2 Cor. 6:2

Jesus was passing by . . . . Then Jesus stopped . . . .

Mt. 20:30, 32

To KNOW AND LOVE the Church, and through the Church
his Mystical Body, to grow in the knowledge and love and
service of Christ, we must be aware of its reality as it exists in
the finitude of human events.

It stands to reason. For just as the word of God, with
divine earnestness, entered and grew in the generative tem-
porality of history, thereby redeeming and transforming it
from its very center, so must his Church develop within
this same particularity.

Simone Weil's condemning of what she termed the "super-
stition of chronology" is utterly alien to the Christian outlook. The Christ whom the Church knows is not only the
Christ of yesterday and tomorrow, but of *today* (Heb. 13:8),
of the palpable *now* that is so often emphasized by the Holy
Spirit (John 12:31). He is the One whom we meet in the
immediacy of the passing moment (Luke 18:3). Christ "who
of God is made unto us wisdom and justice and sanctification
and redemption" (1 Cor. 1:30), *is our Contemporary.*

He is the Christ whom we can touch (Mark 5:28) and
who touches us (Mark 7:33–34; Mt. 8:15). He is not the spurious, unearthly "Christ" of romantic fantasy (a truth bril-
liantly stated by William F. Lynch, S.J., in his "Christ and
Apollo"), but the definite God-made-Man Who lives, not

vii

only with his Father in glory (Eph. 2:6), but in the Church, his pleroma (receiving the plenitude of his grace), that continues his mysteries in the actuality of the time-space process, ever progressing to his triumphant fulfillment (Eph. 4:13).

This is why it is so vital that we sincerely endeavor to know the Church in its concrete duration in which we ourselves are involved, not merely in the abstract, however soaring and magnificent this grandeur, but in its actuality, in our moment, in our place, through which again and again it becomes event, and through which it moves towards the fullness of the Easter mystery. *We cannot truly begin to know it otherwise, for its reality is rooted in our space-time definiteness.* It is subject to a development, a maturation, that allows no rest. It is a life process that moves from stage to stage, with no disregarding of measure, no skipping of the palpable present. In effect, the Church looks to the future coming of the divine Bridegroom, but from within the historic, concrete, immediate moment in which it continues Christ's Incarnation. This is why Karl Rahner, S.J., has the following forthright remarks to say in his excellent book, *The Christian Commitment:*

"In a new age of this kind, which is changing probably far more, not less profoundly than we think, the Church which is in such a world must also, of necessity, be entering into a new epoch, no matter what the Church's prospects in the new age are going to be. This being the case, the Church has got to give thought both to her own nature and to her task in this new age. She must do both; for it is not this age, itself blind and imperilled, which can tell her what she has to do, but only her own nature and her own mandate, eternally ancient and ever new. But reflection on her own nature, in all its fullness and splendor, will not yield any imperative course of concrete action in the pastoral field unless we confront such reflection, boldly and uninhibitedly, with the special character of the new age; unless, then, we have the courage to consider what are the Church's new tasks, and do not turn the theology of the Church into a romantic escape from the crying needs and the special blessings of this age into a cloud-cuckoo land of abstract theology."

What of our contemporary world in which Christ, in his Church, continues his divine mission? What are its special characteristics that distinguish it from other eras, those unprecedented experiences through which, in God's mysterious designs, the Church must advance phase by phase?

It does not require much observation and reflection to realize that our contemporary cosmos is one of fantastic complexity and innovation. Bulldozers, graveyard humanisms, increased mental sickness, the "jet set," canned and frozen foods, global meetings, rock 'n roll, unmanned satellites, military messiahs, transistor radios, hypodermic syringes, canned persuasion, tranquilizers, all the new and strange and wonderful things that speedily become "obsolete"; the proliferation of elaborate organizations that press on all sides; the recurring, widespread loneliness; the cross-currents of unrest that scatter attempts at global peace—all are signs of the profound stirrings within mankind today. The "winds of change" are blowing from many directions, some destructive, bringing with them the "sound of walls crumbling" and the harrowing pain of millions; others creative, shaping new structures and rhythms and dimensions of human existence.

Of course, historical trends do not divide themselves neatly into compartments. They interpenetrate in a complexity that often renders them indistinguishable; and very frequently their movements are so deep below the surface of events that they are hardly discernible. But we may agree with Einstein in his detection of three enormous undertones within today's historical ramifications *: the biological, the atomic (scientific-technological), and the psychological—the "explosions" that now shake our world in staggering transformation. His observation was not exaggerated, for in their impact on our times these three historical trends are decidedly paroxysmal.

* Quoted by Louis and André Rétif in "The Church's Mission in the World"; Volume 102 of the Twentieth Century Encyclopedia of Catholicism.

ACKNOWLEDGMENTS

With grateful acknowledgments to:

SHEED AND WARD, INC., New York, New York, for quotations from: *The Resurrection* by F. X. Durrwell, C.Ss.R., 1960. *The Salvation of Nations* by Jean Danielou, S.J., 1949. *Christ the Sacrament of the Encounter with God* by E. Schillebeeckx, 1963. *The Christian Commitment* by Karl Rahner, S.J., 1963.

FARRAR, STRAUS & GIROUX, INC., New York, New York, for quotations from *The New Man* by Thomas Merton, 1961.

Contents

Today

1 ✳ Humanity Expands

After this I saw a great multitude which no man could number, of all nations, and tribes and peoples and tongues. . . .

Ap. 7:9

The only reason why we take man so absolutely seriously, the only reason why we can, and the reason why (whether we like it or not) we must, is that God, in the Word who became Man, has taken man so absolutely seriously that it is only possible to take God seriously if we take Him seriously as Man, and man, with a divine seriousness, in him.

Karl Rahner

THE BIOLOGICAL SURGE is due in great part to the numerous medical achievements of the past fifty years. Thanks to new drugs and treatments, deaths among infants have dropped precipitously, and the average human life-span is steadily being lengthened. Heart surgery, "miracle" drugs, the successful fight against malaria, smallpox, cholera, plague and other mass killer diseases, organ transplants, plastic artery substitutes, hormones, cobalt bombs—the frontiers of medical science are being pushed forward with spectacular success. And now in the uncharted area of biophysics chemists, biologists, physicists, and even theoretical mathematicians have joined forces to probe further into the mysteries of the human organism and its well-being.

Unquestionably, there are facets of these triumphs that are horrible in their possibilities. Some of the new discoveries effect the most sacredly vital forces of man, and the misuse of such power would set in motion terrifying repercussions. The

3

biological atrocities of Nazism, and the recent thalidomide tragedy were warnings of even more frightful dangers. Huxley's fictitious New Worldian centralized control of reproduction, with its genetic decanting of Betas, Alphas and Alpha Pluses, and the unfortunates subjected to the poisonous "Bokanovsky Process," is a nightmare that spellbinds some individuals, whose will to power would drive them to make it a reality.

Nevertheless, it cannot be denied that a revolutionary era in medicine and medical care has been initiated, one that will be, under the guidance of our Creator, of magnificent promise and fulfillment.

And let us remember that the present "biological explosion" presents not only a luxuriant, physical profusion, but one that is *totally* human: an expansion that embraces imaginative, intellectual and volitional riches as well, an awesome augmentation of human energies that can reach further into the pursuit and realization of Beauty, Truth, Goodness.

And, as Chesterton remarked of St. Francis of Assisi, the Church deliberately does not see the mob for the men, but only the "image of God multiplied, but never monotonous." Each individual person the Mystical Body of Christ respects, honors, and loves, and never allows him to be lost in the chorus of the masses—be it a totalitarianism by violence or welfare, or the type of "hyperdemocracy" that alarms José Ortega y Gasset. For that matter, the Church shares the special compassion of Christ for the multitude (Mt. 15:32), the human, seething "agglomeration" that Ortega y Gasset so disdains.

There is here grandeur of limitless proportions, of which the Church is profoundly aware. Indeed, while recognizing its limitations—in numbers of apostles, the urgent demand for more priests, religious, and militant lay cadres—the Church confronts the overflowing, pulsating human harvest, and welcomes it as one of the signs of the imminent "New Pentecost" boldly announced by Pope John XXIII. Once again *the multitude gathers* (Acts 2:6).

But a crisis is involved. Conditioned especially by the recent advances in medicine and by environmental sanitation, there has been a sudden sharp plummeting of human death rates without a corresponding decline in the very high birth rates, cynically described by Aldous Huxley as a "breeding at random of a viviparous species." According to the best possible estimates, based on historical and archeological evidence, before the discovery of agriculture the total world population was probably less than 20 million. After the Old Kingdom of Egypt it passed 100 million, and reached 500 million towards the close of the seventeenth century. By the middle of the eighteenth century it numbered one billion, and in the 1920's it rose to about two billion. Today the human race is adding to its numbers the equivalent of a good-sized town, more than 90,000 persons, every day—more than the entire population of France annually! At this present rate of acceleration, approaching a two percent annual increase, the human family will have doubled again within sixty years. Forecasters estimate that by the year 2000 as many persons will be added to the global population as were from the time of Adam and Eve until now!

Long term projection into the future cannot, of course, take account of factors that may completely alter conditions. Already it is demonstrable that in the majority of technologically developed countries the voluntary birth rate has fallen rapidly, though in most areas not so fast as the death rate. And Pope Pius XII wisely asked: "Who can be sure that the natural rhythm of procreation will be the same in the future as it is now? Is it not possible that some law moderating the rhythm of expansion from within will come into play?" We must be confident that "Providence has reserved the future destiny of the world to itself," and that Christ's anguished love is ever directed not only to the individual person and to the community, but to the masses, the teeming billions. Nor may we align ourselves with those prophets of doom who, obsessed with the specter of the "population explosion," make hysterical conjectures and crusade for over-simplified, short-term "solutions" that counter God's laws. Pseudo-scientific, statistical clairvoyance, and immoral-amoral patronizing of humanity will not help. But it would be the utmost foolhardiness, and most assuredly unChristian, for us not to recognize the full proportions of the issue bound up with the unparalleled population surge—in the opinion of many, a global problem second only to that of preventing nuclear war. We must not allow ourselves to be content with a Pollyanna optimism or a downright sophomoric indifference.

In the seething context of this biological "explosion," the most formidable task confronting mankind is the provision of enough food for its spiraling numbers. Even now the actual supply is insufficient for two-thirds of the human race who live in the underdeveloped areas of regions of Asia, Africa (including the Middle Eastern countries) and Latin America, the problem continents as far as food production per capita is concerned.

And future prospects? Roughly ten percent of the earth's surface is under cultivation. Twenty percent is pasture land; thirty percent is forest; and forty percent is without agricultural value. With an expansion of crop land and an increase in yields (depending on higher standards of treatment of the cul-

tivable earth through the use of artificial fertilizers and the ro-
tation of crops, and by improved storage and transport) it is
estimated that the agricultural potential of the world may be
three to four times the present production. Furthermore, by
harnessing atomic energy to the desalinization of sea water for
the irrigation of desert areas, specialists foresee a fifty percent
addition to the world's food potential. The further control of
pests and of floods, both feasible today, will also add substantially to this potential. But it must be remembered that these
conclusions are technical and do not take into account tremendous social and economic obstacles.

We must furthermore consider the enormous potential of
the oceans in fish production. The sea covers nearly three-
fourths of the earth, and one acre of it on the average grows
nearly three times as much life, plant and animal, as an acre of
land. But, because of primitive methods of fishing and prejudice, it still provides less than one percent of the world's food.
However, with advance in its understanding and control, pi-
oneered by oceanographers in cooperation with other specialists, we may anticipate a new, rich harvest from the heaving
depths for tomorrow's hungry billions.

Recent chemical processes in our laboratories are also giving
us more sources of foods. Indeed, it is likely that, in the foreseeable future, synthetics will be produced in such large
amounts and at such low costs that the way of life of whole
populations will be dramatically ameliorated.

The intensity and magnitude of the appalling population
crisis is accentuated by the mounting "revolution of expecta-
tions." As pointed out, it is in the undeveloped areas of Asia,
Africa and Latin America, where intolerable hunger, malnutri-
tion and illiteracy prevail, that the highest rate of population

growth (two percent to four percent annually) obtains. Medical "death control" has resulted in the sudden, spectacular fall of death rates, whilst the birth rate continues high. Despite aid and investment from privileged foreign nations, the population increase is outpacing, and in many instances nullifying, the existing efforts to raise the general standard of living. Nor is it possible for these millions to find relief through large-scale emigration, as Europeans did a century or more ago. The consequent frustration of peoples' prospects for human advancement—not only for ample food and clothing and shelter, but for at least the minimum apparatus of modern life, schools, hospitals, means of transportation, etc.—build up burning resentments and pressures that lead to violent, internal revolution or to external aggression or to both. Contemporary history is replete with such eruptions of human desperation that bitterly confront the conscience of all peoples.

2 ✳ The Emergence of Matter

The world is charged with the grandeur of God.
It will flame out, like shining from shook foil;
It gathers to a greatness, like the ooze of oil
Crushed. . . .

There lives the dearest freshness deep down things;
And though the last lights off the black West went
Oh, morning, at the brown brink eastward, springs—
Because the Holy Ghost over the bent
World broods with warm breast and with ah! bright
wings.

Gerard Manley Hopkins, S.J.

Ah, Catholic Church, how utterly I share with you,
In my own way, your passion for the universe!

Paul Claudel

The second "explosion" of our era may well be described as the physical world's "coming of age." Touched by man's genius (upheld by extraordinary asceticism and hard work) profound energies have been released from within the bowels of layered matter, and the mute giant shudders in movement.

Today's Alyosha kisses the earth. His love is not altogether pure: at times he would even prostitute the earth that he embraces. But real love is there too. And not only is his soul awakened; the earth itself rises to new fulfillment.

For as mankind's numbers soar, it simultaneously attains fantastic control over its physical environment. Man has become master of matter, and penetrates it with mind.

In the credos of the eighteenth and nineteenth centuries, man envisaged Nature mechanistically as infinite and absolute, a vast overwhelming reality in which he was submerged. Now he views Nature as measurable and controllable, even though he is more aware of its immense proportions. In the words of Guardini, Nature has become man's "inexhaustible Possibility, Dynamo, Workshop."

Since the application of pure scientific research to technology, a second Industrial Revolution has been triggered, bringing with it the harnessing of new forms of energy and a superabundance of benefits. Extraordinary bursts of inventiveness and dramatic discovery have resulted in the wresting of new forms of energy from the bowels of matter and in channeling them through the conduits of the new City. Increasingly aware of the incredible potentialities inherent in these electronic-atomic-supersonic powers at its disposal, man now hopefully looks beyond his precarious peace to the realization to universal prosperity. Nor are his dreams without foundation. New ways of food and clothing production; new kinds of air-conditioned homes; the construction of cities "of space in light"; new means of travel and entertainment; automatic factories; computers and radio telescopes; astounding accomplishments in surgery; unmanned satellites established at the threshold of the stars, and astronauts waiting to venture on journeys more mysterious than any quest ever visioned by past generations—these are but some of the actualities that point towards the triumphs within mankind's reach.

The rate of this conquest of the universe has been speeded beyond belief. About five thousand years lapsed between the oxcart and sailboat to the invention of the steamboat and locomotive; the next step to the automobile and airplane took about one hundred years; to the coming of the use of the atom, forty years; and to the advent of the sputniks, only twelve years. And as men seek and inquire and test and explore and dare the unknown, this mastering of the universe continues to make its fabulous advance.

Admittedly, there is still the great drama of our time, the terrible disparity between the wealth of the Western World and the poverty of the under-developed countries, and the threatening consequences. The global distribution of the new productivity remains far from realization. There are still the millions of the proletariat who live and work and become unemployed in sub-subsistence conditions. There are still the millions in the grey shadowland of intermediate state of industrialization who reach for survival in the squalor and tragedy of "bidonvilles." But the worldwide "curve toward haveness" is unmistakably rising, a movement towards a universal higher leveling of the standard of human living that is a unique phenomenon of our era. Obstacles to its fulfillment are tremendous, not the least those erected by individuals intoxicated by the will for power and lured by financial wealth; but the spiritual dynamic of the movement, propelled by the recent scientific-technological achievements, is triumphantly active in today's human climate. This is an undeniable fact.

Now, within the avalanche of cumulative, intricate phenomena related to the scientific-technological revolution certain trends of cardinal import are discernible.

One of these Pere Teilhard de Chardin would include in his term "hominization," the process in which man's untapped potentialities find rich fulfillment and whereby he becomes more truly human. Our age is proving that, guided by men dedicated to the pursuit and realization of true humanism, the robot can become an extension of man's total personality, of his very freedom. *"Increased power for increased action; increased action for increased being!"* Chardin's exhilarating vision is already emerging in the reality of history; though slowly it is true, for the forces marshalled against its actualization are many and forbidding.

The first Industrial Revolution was essentially a change in industrial organization, only accidentally a change in industrial techniques. Industrialization, in fact, does not necessarily imply the use of mechanical power. But in our era it does; and in today's Second Industrial Revolution, "an acceleration on top of an acceleration," it is the new supertechniques that stimulate increased complexification in human society and create the needs for more and more organization.

Karl Rahner, S.J., in *The Christian Commitment*, does not hesitate to maintain that the vast possibilities offered by the present scientific-technological advance are such that *their practical realization* cannot be avoided; and that their actualization cannot be accomplished and controlled other than by expanded, organized human effort. In *The New Society* Peter F. Drucker goes further and pinpoints the central hub of this organizing process in the revolutionary principle of mass-production. He sees this principle as absolutely essential to the contemporary scientific-technological industrial system, wherein the individual cannot possibly have access to the highly intricate organizations of men and machines and tools—the "plants" which turn out the collective products. For industrial society only a very small minority of artists and professionals produce independently of such organizations. The principle is so inextricably a part of contemporary existence that it is no longer confined to industrial manufacturing, but has become a pervasive social principle in the organization of human society as a whole.

This phenomenon is, in fact, a symptom of today's impetus in the perennial drive of creation's immensity towards its totalization in man's rich reality as a member of the human collectivity.

However, it is possible—even probable, if responsible leaders are not forthcoming—that this movement of socialization, rising radically from the genuine well-springs of human history, may be temporarily perverted and defected. Instead of developing an organic, vital society, it may well produce an enforced, heterogeneous amalgam, a mechanical fusion of robotized persons.

This grim possibility is already being actualized under Communist totalitarian tyranny. The planned, brutal dehumanization of millions of persons by Red misuse of power is terrifyingly evident—though, the full, abhorrent magnitude of this crime escapes even our wildest imagination.

But it would be a gross mistake for us to believe that the dehumanization of man is limited to such regimes. Most of us fail to perceive the thoroughness of the robotization of the human person that is now being achieved by the streamlined, industrial agglomerations of the "Free World." Coupled with its undeniable benefits, mass-production industry and its present, widespread irresponsible "assembly-line-in-space" technique, has had shattering impact on mankind, especially in those countries that have been recently opened to the scientific-technological advance. Because it is incompatible with so many of the structures and values and satisfactions of traditional society, it has uprooted the human person from the rhythm of life that they had shaped—even in the nucleus of the family. It has treated the worker as "a badly designed single-purpose machine tool," and has divorced him from his work: very often the individual cannot define his contribution to the finished product. It has aggravated the very threat of unemployment, with its psychological as well as physical humiliations; and has thereby augmented the demand for more and more positive, governmental economic action. It has contributed to the build-up of the "power élite," and has made the tragedy of the Big Brother, Totalitarian State an imminent possibility.

In sum, we must concede that our near-autonomous realms of industry, and the marginal environs associated with them, not infrequently tend to suffocate the human personality in an all-pervasive, almost imperceptible process of a devitalizing, so-called "dynamic conformity," that sucks at its inmost reality. The process may be meticulously hygienic and cushioned ("politely and inconspicuously," observed Huxley), but the eventual deformation of man is every bit as thorough as that achieved by "Authoritarian Technology." The automaton, whatever the method of re-creation in the image of the Blueprint, is an automaton, is an automaton, is an automaton. . . . .

And the robotized person is also being urbanized. The phenomenon of rapid organization is one of the most remarkable features of contemporary, industrialized human existence. For example: between 1800 and 1950 the population of Buenos Aires leapt from 40,000 to 3,200,000—an increase of 8,000 percent in 150 years! True, there is no simple and straight correlation between industrialization and urbanism; but it definitely favors the City. All existing data indicate that the new scientific-technological progress has contributed enormously to the accelerated urbanization of very recent times, and continues to do so. Whilst the process is not, in itself, planned (though the symbolic "Brasilia" may well be the pilot for many more such schemes), its culmination, always in a state of mobility, gives rise to new, complex, organized patterns of human existence, many voluntary, others obligatory. The process ineluctably fans out, even into the small rural communities dominated by agricultural interests.

Now, socialization as such must not be identified with crowd standardization, with political socialism or with economic collectivism. Essentially, it is the striving of humanity towards the fulfillment of its untapped irreducible qualities by means of corporate organization in whose union the individual members become more differentiated and strengthened in their being.

Thus, it is no passing coincidence that our era witnesses a widespread resurgence of interest (sometimes regrettably, blindly fanatical) in cultural identification, and the emergence of formerly colonized peoples into civic responsibility and nationhood (also frequently accompanied by tragic bitterness and violence); for the movement towards mankind's unification is also, paradoxically, an increase in its authentic differentiation.

But it is obvious that socialization presents immeasurable dangers as well as opportunities. When guided by men acting by God's wisdom as contained in the dictates of the Natural Law and, above all, in his revealed Word, it can help mankind to new heights commensurate with its stupendous destiny. It can also lead not only to political over-centralization and the swallowing of small enterprise in the avaricious maw of mass production controlled by a "Power Elite," but to the ghastly horror and degradation of collective death camps. Orwell's 1984 is no mere piece of nightmarish fantasy. As Huxley puts it, "the practical, depersonalized, mechanistic reduction of human diversity to subhuman uniformity, the 'social engineering' of human beings who are reduced to mere reflex entities, can amount to nothing other than a hideous hell-on-earth."

Whatever the temporary perversions, true socialization contributes to mankind's profound advance toward global pluralistic unification. Moreover, as mankind's spiraling numbers, spatially confined (so far!) to a spherical planet, become more and more compact, mutually influential, and interdependent, and inevitably more organized, the new media of communication augment and hasten the universal rapprochement in astounding measure. Modern communications—by transportation and by audio-visual techniques—have encircled the globe and are broadening people's knowledge of one another and of the over-all space-time environment in which all dwell. They engender a human confluence that is not only geographical, but psychological. The worldwide physical convergence is, in fact, but a structure for the spiritual communion of all human beings. Accordingly, "relationships are forming which go beyond the horizons of the province and the nation, in order to reach the human scale: a communal humanism, a universal civilization."

The human family has known dreamers who have looked beyond its fragmentation to a harmonious future—as does the Church in its eschatological orientation. For the Church is aware that the original human unity was disrupted by sin: Origen's *"Ubi peccato, ibi multitudo"* succinctly expresses its tradition. As such, the restoration of mankind's unity is its most cherished aspiration; for, as de Lubac emphasized in his great work *Catholicism,* the communion of mankind in the Mystical Body of Christ presupposes a pristine natural solidarity of the human race in the first Adam. Out of inter-individual and international integration Christ can fashion an infinitely surpassing, supernatural unity, and so effect the peace that He alone can bring (John 14:27).

It is interesting to note that there are profound energies directed towards international unification already geared to motion within the rhythm of our contemporary life. The recent Internation Geophysical Year was a splendid, ambitious scientific collaboration symptomatic of these orientations. There are also the beginnings of a profound dialogue between East and West.

But the realization of harmonious human progress will necessitate far more than intermittent pooling of efforts pressed in the service of humanity. Global unity evidently entails deeper inter-communion and constant cooperation; and this demands sacrifice, the stripping of the various types of exclusiveness, personal, local and national, that militate against human welfare. Such ordered collaboration, with its mutual relationships of trust and esteem between peoples, can be achieved and maintained only through Christ present in human history through the sacramental organism of his Mystical Body, of which we are members—and as such, called to be, through grace, "artisans of the union of human hearts." The grim alternative will continue to be division, dissension, total nuclear armaments and the menacing horror of wholesale annihilation.

Before concluding our short study of the scientific-technological "explosion" we must not omit mention of the leisure gained by the use of the supermachine. The explosive increase in leisure is still confined, for the most part, to North American and parts of European society, but with the spread of computer-operated industrialization it is fast becoming worldwide. For automation is fast eliminating the need for human work hours, and the resulting leisure is growing faster than man's present capacity to use it wisely. The leisure vacuum is usually filled with a "recreation" that dissipates rather than re-creates: instead of being a deliverance, an opportunity for personal unfolding and enrichment, it becomes a barren boredom that exhausts and warps. One economist in the United States observes that within ten years' time it may be necessary to keep the leisured population under more or less constant sedation if they cannot be given something better to do! Indicative of the seriousness of the situation is the setting up of a special standing committee for the study of leisure by the American Psychiatric Association.

The leisure boom is, in effect, one of the many problems whose basic variables have to be investigated and resolved if the "hominization" of man by the use of scientific-technological accomplishments is to continue—a colossal enterprise that will require not only studies that represent applied mathematics, physics and chemistry, and involve bio-medical behavioral techniques, but also demand, and urgently, the wisdom of philosophy and theology.

We must realize that the Church seeks to purify and assimilate the scientific-technological civilization that is being erected. It is acutely aware of the dangers involved: the fact remains that mankind's new push-button, demiurgic power is full of problem and danger as well as of magnificent prospect. It can provide H-bombs as well as tractors; it can enslave humanity under planetary bombardment and bring it to the very fringes of hell, or break the limitations of time and space and extend his freedom.

But Christ's Mystical Body is confident in divine Providence, and recognizes the great good that wells up within mankind. "The energy with which modern man seeks to understand, dominate and utilize nature, putting it at his service, must be considered a worthy response to the endowment given man by God." (Pope Paul VI.) The Church knows that the New Babylon can, by man's effort partnered with God's grace, reflect the New Jerusalem.

The Cenacle has expanded, as Claudel observed, and now coincides with the entire universe. *Once again the multitude gathers together in the City* (Acts 2), *this time for a new Pentecost.*

It would be well here to inject an inference that will have enormous bearing in our brief look at the so-called "psychological explosion."

Undeniably, our world is in ferment. Our era is experiencing an extraordinary hastening of historical development. The past half century has produced more social upheavals—of vastly enlarged dimensions—than the preceding centuries; and the pace is quickening. Mankind is suddenly swept along in an increasing, frenzied momentum towards a future of awesome possibilities.

But, as already noted by Cardinal Suhard in 1946, the

unique features of this upsurge of intense change cumulatively indicate that *we live in an era of crucial transition*. The "modern" period of history is consummated, and out of the unleashed pain and destruction a world with new structures and new rhythms to human existence is in growth, in actual formation. This is no arbitrary platitude, one that we may summarily dismiss with the wry comment that the words "we live in an age of transition" were originally spoken by Adam to Eve after their dismissal from Eden. It is a fact established by the convergent phenomena that we have been summarily analyzing.

However, we must not make the mistake of reducing our era to the dimensions of a mere product of past history and a dispensable scaffolding for the future. It has ineluctable meaning in itself, a providentially indispensable role to play in God's mysterious designs. Our time is not merely a time of waiting, as Paul Tillich declared. As we shall see, it has unique values to contribute (with our cooperation) to the building up of Christ's Mystical Body—the terminus of all history.

No doubt, we must view our time within the perspectives of past events and of future possibilities and probabilities. But we must also attempt to see it in its own, immediate, complex character—and embrace it with a redeeming love.

It is our era. It permeates our innermost being. It is our responsibility.

3 ✳ Nacht und Nebel*

I am the fear that frightens me!
I am the desert of despair!
And the night of agony!

James Stephens

I don't know. I'll never know, in the silence
you don't know, you must go on, I can't go on,
I'll go on.

Samuel Beckett

For men are homesick in their homes,
And strangers under the sun.
And they lay their heads in a foreign land
Whenever the day is done.

G. K. Chesterton

THE THIRD "explosion" mentioned by Einstein to the Abbé
Pierre would more inclusively be called "spiritual" rather than
psychological; for it embraces the whole range of human spirit.

Today's dazzling mutation of mankind's physical environment is little compared to the unprecedented metamorphosis
within mankind itself. The interior newness of man is far
more extraordinary than all the myriad, recent, external
changes lumped together. Actually, their combined orientation converges in the human spirit.

Their impart has opened up mankind's horizons to staggering proportions. Paleontology, ethnology and kindred sciences,

* Night and Fog: First words of Alberich's incantation in Wagner's
"The Ring of the Nibelungs," which, when he wore his helmet, enabled
him to disappear, being replaced by a column of fog; and in Nazi concentration camps the words designating a class of youths to be used as
guinea pigs in scientific experiments. (François Mauriac)

project his awareness backward in time to his remote origins: the physical sciences project his awareness forward into vistas that extend limitlessly from the abysses of the atom to the depths of the sea, to the reaches of space. For the first time in its history mankind, no longer earthbound, is enabled to measure itself in the full sweep of cosmic reality. With the increasing freedom from material limitations, the individual person is offered means for increased freedom from spiritual enfoldment through greater understanding and betterment of self and of the universal human solidarity. Now, moved from a restricted environment into one of many more creative human possibilities, he is forced to choose, to determine, to grow in non-transferable responsibility. And with the new expansion in beauty (the beauty that Dostoievsky perceived would play a considerable role in mankind's salvation), he is invited to attune his sensibilities to the emergence of created loveliness.

In effect, the present historical situation is an opportunity for an unparalleled maturation of the human spirit—one that is receiving tremendous response from mankind, as evidenced in the widespread, determined expression of massive yearnings, not only for bread and TV, but for effective recognition of human dignity, for freedom, for the full stature of the human personality.

Simultaneous with mankind's spiritual awakening have been the remarkable developments in psychotherapy. Man is now able to look more deeply into the various subterranean "levels" of his soul. As Josef Goldbrunner has pointed out, he now has the opportunity to explore and fulfill the conditions necessary for "wholeness" of human existence. Knowing himself more thoroughly with the assistance of the new depth-psychology, he can the better orientate his efforts (in union with God's grace) toward self-realization. Karl Stern does not hesitate to refer to these advances as revolutionary in the history of the human spirit: for they constitute a new light that can help mankind's journey through the darkness of neurotic and psychotic affliction, and enlighten him in the maintenance of health of soul. However, these same insights into man's psychic make-up also provide fatal possibilities for the systematic manipulation of men's minds, as well as their reflex and nervous systems—an alarming fact that has already been demonstrated by the hybrid techniques of Communist "brain-washing."

The spirit of contemporary man is, in fact, a prey to a dreadful mélange of forces that threaten the equilibrium of his innermost being—that tend, in fact, to make him abnormally normal, adjusted, as he should not be, to a world society that is (in this historically transitional period of constant flux and metamorphosis) to an incredible degree inhuman.

Here we deal with imponderables, but if we interpret aright, the following short analysis, while far from being comprehensive, indicates the major "maladies of the soul" that stalk mankind, making ours an era of neuroses.

"It is fear, here in this house." Alan Paton's words in *Cry, the Beloved Country* are applicable not only to the people of South Africa, torn by disastrous interracial strife, but to the entire human family as it experiences the trauma of a world in convulsion. Already a generation ago Karl Jasper wrote that fear, "unparalleled in its intensity, is modern man's sinister companion." For mankind is now confronted by fantastic perspectives and possibilities that grip its spirit in piercing anxiety: the "enormity of space," * the limitless, awesome spread of the universe; the "enormity of duration,"* the ceaseless flux of events that speed toward a hidden future; the "enormity of

* Expressions used by Teilhard de Chardin.

number,"* the shattering milliards of beings surrounding the individual human person who seeks identity; and, in addition, the scandal of interlocked, deadlocked Big Powers, with their arsenals of apocalyptic bombs, and the spectre of universal obliteration. As Guardini observed, henceforth, since the advent of nuclear weapons and the possibility of planetary suicide, mankind will experience in its depth a new, unique fear. "Since Hiroshima, we know that we live on the rim of disaster, and that we shall stay there till the end of history." Now, indeed, international "peace" amounts to an "uneasy interlude existing precariously by virtue of the balance of mutual fright . . . a balance of armed fear."

Certainly there is a healthy fear that attends man's awareness of the darkness from which he has been created and near to which he always remains. But this wholesome disquietude is altogether different from the prevalent anxiety that is bound up with the cancellation of God and of the virtue of hope, and with an elusive, neurotic guilt.

Contemporary man is haunted by insecurity. In an era of staggering complexity and of accelerated new sensations, images, ideas and questions, he is confronted by all kinds of concrete situations that must be sorted out and classified by him, and to which he must react. He is, to an unprecedented degree, at the mercy of social, economic and political vagaries and fluctuations. He must learn new reflexes and steel himself to the multiplicity of shocks that come his way without respite. But adjustment comes only with the utmost effort, and only when the individual person has guidance and reassurance from dependable authority—precisely the lamentable need among the majority of people who, lacking in convictions, drift on a sea of shifting opinions.

Contemporary man often hides his insecurity behind masks

such as a "mystique" of speed, a wild hyperactivity, an insatiable pursuit of novelty, an evasion of the complexity of reality, an aggressive self-assertion, or an abandonment to the urge of domination—all forms of frustrating escapism. But his sense of agonizing uncertainty becomes more pronounced.

Moreover, there is the phantom of loneliness, of an anguished sense of desolation that borders on the pathological. Not infrequently contemporary man suffers from an uprootedness that crushes his spirit to near breaking point. He is lured and forced from his rural community and left among strangers (competitors) in the anonymous, cosmopolitan City; he is hurried from his ancestral heritage and, detribalized, lost; he is displaced from his native country and sent wandering. Often he is estranged from his work, from older and younger generations, and even from the center of his own being. On the ontological level he is endangered by being exiled from his past and present.

And this alienation is worsened by the irresponsible manipulation of human sensibilities by the many mass media, particularly radio and television, that progressively blanket our cultures. Seduced by their banal fantasies, man's soul, already without sufficient anchorage in God (and thereby in the plenitude of created being), is given more and more a hollow dilution of what is real. Instead of becoming imbued with the strong presence of being, it must eventually feed on its own poverty—and the existential solitariness and depression deepen.

Living in an increasingly affluent society, contemporary man is tempted to surrender himself hedonistically to the fatal enchantment of temporal goods. He is buffeted by a frenzy of sensations. His daily life is fragmented into a multiplicity of the merely contingent.

The physical biological "explosions" tend to glut his spirit in a tumult of palpable stimulants that combine to form a kind of carnal cosmos. He is so gorged by the juices of physical creation that his very sensitivity to the nuances of sensations often becomes numbed: all he experiences are ice-cold bubbles. The assault is such that the yielding to the unbridling of one's instincts is widely considered the only normal thing to do.

Moreover, plunged in a world of impersonal relativity, one so markedly lacking in spiritual joy, many persons abandon themselves to the ecstasy of pleasure in a tragic search for an absolute, for identity, and for love. They drown themselves "in the spray of phenomena," in a self-squandering, frantic "plenitude of the moment."

Associated with this unchaining of instincts is a peculiar loathing for all that authentically relates to God and to man's supernatural welfare. Superstitions, veneered with sophistication, and erotic, narcissistic "mysticisms" abound: but the disgust that the monks of the East called *acedia*, the nauseating "tristitia de bono spirituali," reminiscent of the Israelites' loathing of the manna (Nm. 1:5), weighs on man's spirit.

And behind the ennui and dissonances of this naturalism, stirs a muffled nostalgia for innocence.

At least in one respect Heraclitus of ancient Greece would find our present global climate of extraordinary interest, for never before has change, flux, been so dramatically in evidence nor so widely accepted as a value in itself. The capricious fascination of novelty has so fevered contemporary man's spirit that in delirium he has elevated it to the realm of absolutes. And the results are disastrous. Cultural tradition, with its continuity, its lessons, and its riches, is increasingly neglected; and human existence is littered with things outmoded—even though they were brought into our lives but yesteryear, yesterday. Every dawn must bring a shower of new foods, new song "hits," new news, new "kicks," even new "friends" and new "situation" ethics. (*Neugier* "hunger for the new.") It would appear that the ideal is to erect "a civilization based on obsolescence." While this is particularly true of North American technological society, the craze is fast spreading.

But because of the composite nature of his person, man is radically "tactile" on every level of his being: he cannot survive humanly in an historical vacuum. To develop his potentialities, he needs the support and the stimulus of the history that preceded him and that now surrounds him; and, in turn, he must react by contributing to its growth. One is reminded of the recent experiments wherein volunteers were deprived, even for a very short time, of all sensory stimuli, and "little by little their brains went dead or slipped out of control," and various pathological symptoms developed. In an analogous manner, when contemporary man moves in the isolation of passing novelties, and fails to "touch" history, his uprootedness takes on frightening dimensions.

In this connection Father William Lynch's comments on the American Romantic Hero ("New Adam") complex are of great import. The image of the archetypal Adam provided the early pioneers with an orientation, a mystique, that urged them on to brave tremendous risks and achieve further conquests. This mentality of the person of newness without any obligation whatsoever to hampering past history, "self-reliant and self-propelling, ready to confront whatever awaited him with the aid of his own unique and inherent resources" contributed no small share to the realization of their adventure.

But in our day, instead of giving due place to the necessity

and value of tradition, it demands again and again fresh beginnings; rather than liberating the American character, it tends to
hamper its development. Our culture has become a one-gener-
ation, even an annual, rebirth of a completely brand new Phoe-
nix in "blooming, buzzing confusion."

The burden of harassment that this complex imposes on the
human spirit—particularly that of youth—is crushing, often
beyond endurance. Pressured not only by the impact of the
novelties themselves, but also by the fear of being damned as
outsiders, persons submerge themselves in desperate élan.
And iconoclasm becomes a virtue.

Undoubtedly, one of the most insidious threats to the
health of contemporary man's spirit is the fetid atmosphere of
scepticism as expressed, for instance, in the spew of "black lit-
erature" of our time, with its obsession with decadence and it
rhetoric of revulsion. There is not a little romantic, rhetor-
ical, humbug and masochism in the new philosophies of negation. Bataille's affected "I refuse to be happy!" scowls from
many narcissistic corners of the contemporary Dark Night.
But the real anguish of unsought scepticism is also present,
and abounds.

Sophisticated, contemporary man pictures all humanity in
the guise of the god-like Cartesian Centaur, who rode into history in the seventeenth century on an impeccable Newtonian
machine, and who is now hopelessly ill and dismembered, his
machine a thing of infernal destruction. Unlettered, with Jons
in Bergman's movie, The Seventh Seal, he is tempted to con-
clude simply that "everything is worth precisely as much as a
belch." The meaningless and absurd become absolute; any real
affirmation is instinct with the ironic.

He is surrounded on all sides by the "sound of walls crumbling." So many of his ideals have come to grief. Truths are

pilloried in vitriolic versatility, and far too often those who defend them do so with ponderously delivered platitudes that are capable of evoking nothing but vehement scorn. Traditional principles of morality are hurled aside as shackling taboos of an unenlightened past; and again, far too often, those who are elected to guide society are unmasked in their own pretensions and corruption.

Enmeshed in this welter of devaluation, contemporary man is tempted to be finally convinced that left under the control of traditional norms, our world will remain a featureless, neutral sort of place; an arid landscape of ruins despite the monotonous façade of modern progress, inhabited by entombed human marionettes who are beguiled by myths and bawdy innuendoes of eternity, and whose lives suffer intolerable emptiness.

He has, therefore, developed an intense awareness of life's darkness, an atmosphere in which there is no mutual trust; in which things terrible often seem natural, and things natural appear terrible; and wherein people die with indifference and kill with indifference.

Thus poisoned by the swill of scepticism, contemporary man often decided that his only responses to human existence as it is today should be either paralyzing escapism in the meaningless vitality of the moment, or the fury of wild rebellion, now "one of the essential dimensions of man."

Neither alternative is creative. Both destroy.

Contemporary man has a bogus religion of the exchurched and unchurched—Culture, with its absolute either Science (as consecrated by Augustus Comte) or Art (as divinized by Matthew Arnold), both extensions of his own self. He is the Priest of the most recent scientific symbols and of the "eternal imagination," in whose liturgies he creates a Divinity in his own image.

Without doubt, the most infernal force now pulling at man's spirit is this "Dionysian (or Wellsian) Temptation" to make himself God. Contemporary man is drunk with power —whether he be the statesman or business executive with enormous control over persons and things, or the youth careening down the highway in the geared-up automobile. He can bend matter and its energies to his service; he has access to vast new realms of existence. In the intoxication of simulated omnipotence he can (at any rate for limited periods of time) forget the deep wounds in his being and deafen himself to the cosmic rumblings of danger that encompass him, and the intimations of eternity that haunt him. He is offered the world —ultimately, at the price of a nightmarish, temporal "paradise" closed to all that is transcendent, and an eternal damnation—and in Promethean defiance, he rebels against a transcendent God.

Environmental climate intensifies the temptation to self-deification. For Western Man, renegade to his Christian vocation, has to a very great extent desacralized the universal civilization that is fast encircling the globe. His experiment of "Genesis in reverse," begun some four hundred years ago, has been highly successful (though not producing the triumphant happiness that he had defiantly predicted). Despite the catastrophies, the myriad achievements point to more astounding possibilities—and man is tempted to proclaim in blasphemy a salvation of man by man, within a universe stripped of mystery, shaped by mathematical abstractions, shut off from the very breath of God. "My faith is in the possibilities of man!" (Julian Huxley). Unaided by the Spirit of God he, and not the Church, would mold a truly catholic civilization; and his conquests in the material world would become his mystical body. Paradoxically, contemporary man, whilst running desperately from his own fear, "having looked more deeply into the mystery of evil than most generations before" (Paul Tillich), is nevertheless tempted to ape the Almighty, to take to himself the functions of the Holy Spirit.

Assailed by these forces that threaten his very soul, contemporary man's new access to the "deep cellar" of his being is fraught with dangers. Father William F. Lynch, S.J., warns of "the growing Manichean sense among us, the excessive sense of evil in our nature and in things outside of us. It breeds guilt, but it is the kind that leads to submission . . . never a submission to God or the truth, but to anything. It becomes a disease of submission to anything"—and, tragically, it is intensified by man's exploration of his soul without guidance dictated by God's light.

Moreover, there are drugs now being manufactured that can control irrational behavior and induce normal behavior—new achievements of chemistry that may, when used unscrupulously, induce terrifying desecration to man's spirit. Even the chemically induced happiness of Huxley's wonder drug "soma" ("all the advantages of Christianity and alcohol; none of their defects") already seems less fictitious; and its perils seem nearer.

There is one other aspect of the present historical situation that we must bear in mind, for its significance is paramount. It is the *youth* of our time, the center and the heart of humanity, whose spirit is most acutely affected by the great upheavals and mutations. They are the most sensitive to the relentlessly changing physical environment, and to the bewildering ubiquitous relativity, intellectual, moral and religious, that inflicts incalculable harm on their interior life. All too frequently those who should guide them through the instability and insecurity are themselves suffering from loss of spiritual equilibrium: confused by the most recent questionings of values and pedagogical methods, they have abdicated authority. And so, denied proper guidance and inspiration, youth are in revolt against the complex environment whose pervasive, suffocating nihilism wearies their exuberance and idealism. Their thirst for life and their search for identity find expression in scattered revolt against society, in a cult of independence and personal experience, in an escape into abrupt, brutal sensations, in a cynical realism, in the effectiveness of action, in group conformism, in sincere, groping contemplation—even in heroic (sometimes to the summit of martyrdom), often quixotic service to their fellow man in an age wherein so many persons die with indifference.

We must mark this well, we who have betrayed the "young barbarians" and who decry them: contemporary youth, whose entrance into adulthood is abnormally delayed because of numerous social circumstances, and whose numerical growth is accelerated phenomenally, are truly the "silent revolution" whose vital, bursting impact on the shaping of our emerging world will be of momentous consequences, and it is they who, energized by the Holy Spirit, will have the duty and privilege of actualizing the "Second Pentecost."

Undoubtedly it appears that mankind is succumbing more and more to the squandering and loss of its spiritual caliber. But may we not see in today's gropings and agonies and perversions of the human spirit a terrible, hallowing, furrowing and purification of man's soul?

Since the Renaissance, as Freud expressed it, man has been "insulted," pushed further back by the Cosmic revolution

initiated by Copernicus, by the Biological revolution sparked
by Darwin, by the Cultural revolution ignited by Marx, and
by the Psychological revolution introduced by Freud himself. Despite—and because of—the speed and uproar that
surrounds him, man has been pushed deeper within his own
being, sometimes to discover unfathomed wealth, often to
find the void, the vortex. But the phenomenon is unmistakable: whilst embracing more of the external world, man is
simultaneously retreating into his own mystery.

There is no longer the house of the first Pentecost (Acts
2:1–4), but there is the movement of contemporary man to
within his own spiritual recesses, into the interior room of his
spirit, wherein he confronts not only the meaning of his own
selfhood, but that of the vast human community.

May we not view it as a preparation for—even the inauguration of—the "New Pentecost," an extraordinary working of the
Holy Spirit within the innermost zones of humanity? Living in
the "time of the Church" we are involved in the continuation
of the Pentecostal mystery. But there are moments in history
when the Holy Spirit bestows divine grace in exceptional outpourings. And ours is such a moment. The Finger of God
(Luke 11:20) probes with burning, healing deftness within
the torn entrails of mankind. At the center of the hurricane
fury of our world in travail remains the eye of deep calm from
which the Paraclete radiates his divine power.

4 ✳ History: Sacred—Profane

*Since Easter, human time has been advancing
towards an event of the past, the Resurrection of
Christ, and it will only reach it at the end of history.*

*Our Lord has passed out of our time and become
its center because He is its fullness, its master because He is its end . . . This, then, is the road
taken by the Church as a whole and in her members:
she starts from the Resurrection of Christ and moves
towards the Resurrection of Christ, progressing in
her participation in divine life until she is wholly
filled by it. In the final glorification the association
with the Resurrection which began at baptism will
be consummated: the Church will be "glorified with
Him," glorified in the same act that glorifies her
Savior. Thus the Church is moving towards an event
which historically happened before she existed, the
event of Easter.*

F. X. Durwell, C.S.S.R.

THE MULTIFARIOUS, onthrusting process that we have been
studying may be termed secular history: the chronological series of human events, the *motio physica* of cultural, political
and economic phenomena—the history that, contemplated
outside the perspectives of supernatural faith, "forms a picture
of most fearful aspect, and excites the profoundest emotions
and the most hopeless sadness" (Hegel). We have not been
so much concerned with the surface waves as with the hidden
coalescence of underlying currents, the forces that are trans-
muting both the universe and the individual persons and
human collectivity inserted into it.

Now, the deepest meaning of this "profane" history consists
in its being a preparation, a prolegomenon, for sacred history:
that is, history in its most profound sense, the unfolding of
God's economy of Salvation, the cosmic movement of supernatural happenings that reaches from time into eternity—
indeed, brings eternity, the reality to come, into time.

These two histories are distinct and distinguishable by reason of their nature, but they are inextricably intertwined in the profound complexity of human existence. We live in both these historical processes; or rather—a truth of capital importance—both advance in us.

Let us anticipate and consider briefly the progressive development of sacred history. This should help us locate our separate meditations in the totality of our study.

Before Christ there extended the great period of readiness, the cosmic Advent replete with the *mirabilia Dei*, the wonderful works of Yaweh, and the awesome "drama of the forerunners" that anticipated and prefigured in type the approach of the God-Man.

Then, in the fullness of time, history achieved its purpose. In Christ, its terminus, specifically in his Resurrection, the New Creation to come was already inaugurated.

Finally, in the present phase of sacred history, these "last times," the "time-between," in which we live, in which we shape and are being shaped, the Church, Christ's mystical continuation, moves to its completion; that is, to the ultimate manisfestation of the divine victory already accomplished in the Son of Man, and to the eternal rejuvenescence of mankind and the entire cosmos.

In other words, the Church, Spouse of the *Kyrios*, strives to hasten the Second Coming of the Divine Bridegroom. And it brings nearer the Parousia by continuing, with holy urgency, the mission of the Son of God: the redemption and divinization of fallen humanity by the interior communication of grace.

The Church, divine society transcendent to contingency, remains a visible Body plunged into secular history. In its temporal reality it is "subject to the vicissitudes of centuries and the laws of human societies." This rooting in time and space is necessary, by divine dispensation, for the Church's growth and purgation. Thereby involved in secular history—the history that undergoes divine judgment—the Church penetrates the secular process, purifying, assimilating and transforming it in Christ. The Church, in the present phase of sacred history, the "last hour" (1 John 2:18), the very embodiment of this history, enters into secular history by an "ascending," redemptive incarnation, assuming all its complex reality except sin. It is successively incarnated, in the image of the incarnation of the Word, in the movement of all authentic human values: each culture, each age, our own included, lends the Church "its stature and countenance." Analogous to Mary's immaculate contribution to the making of Christ's humanity, mankind today—the contemporary mankind we have been considering—contributes the material (crass and dirtied, but redeemable) that providentially goes to incarnate Christ in our immediate historical context.

As we shall see later in more detail, our Christian mission is to be so rooted in the authentic values of here-and-now so that, guided by the Holy Spirit and overshadowed by the power of the Most High (Luke 1:35), we can participate in the building up of the Whole Christ.

Thus we are destined to become makers of history—of total history, both sacred and secular. After the apocalyptic manner of the Prophets of the Old Testament, we are to take the initiative right in the center of history's tremendous advance!

Renewal

5 * Pasch

Christ, Our Passover, has been sacrificed!

1 Cor. 5:8

And I, if I be lifted up from the earth, will draw all things to myself.

John 12:32–33

If, then, any man is in Christ, he is a new creature: the former things have passed away; behold, they are made new!

2 Cor. 5:17

WE HAVE STATED that to know and love Christ, we must know and love him in his Church of our historical situation; for the Church is the Lord mystically present in our concrete immediacy, in Today (Heb. 3:13). This, precisely, is the astounding mystery that remained hidden in God from eternity, and that is now revealed in these last times (Eph. 3; 1 Cor. 2:7).

We will examine this truth in more detail; for, indeed, the fact of the mystical, redeeming, transforming passage of the Word of God through our total space-time duration is the kernel to our meditation. But we must bear in mind that, even though we were to devote lengthy study to it (which is beyond the scope of our present effort), we should say much "and yet shall want words" (Sir. 43:29). For it is the focus of all mysteries.

So far, our special concern has been secular history. Like Paul Valéry, our interest has been the sea, the deep, strong undercurrents of contemporary history, not the surface foam of events.

Here we turn to sacred history, the spiritual cosmos of vast grandeur that lifts mankind up into immense perspectives, and provides its tortuous advance with meaning.

Now, all history, both sacred and profane, has its origin in the One who is First and Last, the Alpha and Omega (Is. 48:12), the beginning of all things and their end (Apoc. 1:18), "Who created Heaven and the things that are therein, and the earth and the things that are therein, and the sea and the things that are therein" (Apoc. 10:6), and he is not the mere "God" of the philosopher's abstract formula, but the personal, numinous Triune God, who is consuming fire of love (Heb. 12:29). He is "Lord of hosts" (Is. 14:4), before whom the sea flees and the mountains skip like rams and the rocks turn into pools of water (Ps. 113:3–8) and the earth trembles (Jgs. 5:3–5). Yet he is Parent and Redeemer (Is. 63:16), whose very Name is Hope (Ps. 135:12). He is the Father and Son and Holy Spirit (1 John 5:7–8), the awesome life of "perpetual movement of flux and reflux, the Unity forever going outwards into the Trinity, and the Trinity forever drawing together into Unity" (Ruysbroeck); the most perfect community of the most radical, personal individuality.

Already, before the creation of the cosmos, God has predestined mankind in his son. And then, Revelation tells us, in the beginning of time, the Almighty, in infinite, lavishing love, and with unfathomable magnaminity, brought humanity out of dark nothingness, and destined to "pour out his Spirit upon it, and to give to it the adoption of sons" (St. Irenaeus). He proposed that all persons, whom he created in the pattern of his Son, the substantial Image of his substance (Heb. 1:3), and whom he loves individually with a unique, personal love, should be partakers of His divine nature (2 Pt. 1:4) in a human race united with the divine will and within itself. Then came the frightening impasse of mankind's fall from grace.

For man, in absurd, blasphemous revolt, chose death and disintegration. "He wanted to make himself his own center" (Pascal). By the sin of Adam and Eve, in whom we all confronted our Creator, humanity was sundered from communion with divine life, and its own oneness was disrupted. Death entered into man's experience (Gn. 3:19), and the "one nature was shattered into a thousand pieces" (Maximus the Confessor).

In effect, mankind, in the blind smugness of sin, disregarded the superbeing and transcendent unity of divine adoption (Rom. 8:12–17; 1 Jn. 3:1), and settled for a deprived, decaying existence—like that of the disinherited, disenchanted cosmos of Beckett's seedy solipsist, in which "the sun shone, having no alternative, on, the nothing new . . . :" the captive empire of death (Heb. 2:15).

Notwithstanding, there persists the fact that remains absurd and unbelievable to human logic: God still loved man, the eviscerated non-hero, with a "relentless" love whose purity and fidelity would surmount the infernal negation of evil. Like the demon-ridden Kirillov, every single one of us can cry out: "God has pursued me all my life!"—pursued with love. For the divine charity does not depend on our response (1 Jn. 4:9–10): God loves mankind wholly because He is Love (1 Jn. 3:8–9). As a matter of fact, all that is good and lovable in us has its eternal origin in the Trinity.

It is in Christ that the Almighty designed to reconcile mankind to himself (2 Cor. 3:18). The God-Man would be the one Mediator between the Triune Holiness and estranged human-

ity (1 Tm. 2:5). He would be the cause of eternal salvation
(Heb. 5:10) through the sacrifice of his own self (Heb.
9:27, 38).

This "Christ-event" necessitated preparation, a unique ped-
agogy by way of accustoming men to the Word, and the
Word himself to men (St. Irenaeus).

Already in pre-Israelite times, the Divine Bridegroom was
wooing humanity, entering into a Covenant through Noe with
all nations (Act. 14:15), and sealing it with the multi-colored
testimony of the rainbow (Gen. 9:8–12). The Father, who is
Silence, whispered through the Word, who is Expression, in
the innermost depths of man's being (John 1:9). And from
within the teeming torrent of created reality he offered to
those who, in reverence like Melchisedech, would truly, sacramentally see and hear and smell and taste and touch his creation, an obscure, but real confirmation of their interior religious experience. They could find it in the effulgence of
golden light, and in the surging sea and lonely immensity of
desert and towering rock, and in sun-ripened grapes and bursting melons, and in sound, and in limpets and earwigs and
heifers and chattering starlings—and in man himself, the
priest of creation, whose splendor, as Pascal reminds us, is discernible even in his wretchedness. For all are the myriad,
transparent "sacraments of nature," the hollowed cosmic "image of the Image," that remains opaque only to the dreary
foolishness of the proud (Rom. 1:20; Acts 14:14–16).

This was the pre-Biblical, universal religion of the natural
universe, in which the upright heathen, *in tenebris*, despite
many perversions and aberrations, polytheism and anthropo-
morphism, attained intuition of Divine Providence working in
their midst, and lived by its guidance.

But the Bridegroom (Os. 2:16–19) moved closer to mankind; for humanity had, strangely, wounded the divine heart with a shaft of love (Canticle of Canticles 4:9; Ps. 8:3–8). Yahweh, the One, Holy God, now intervened in human history and assembled a scattering of unknown tribes, bringing the Israelite nation into existence (Ez. 16:3–13; Gen. 12:1–3). Through Abraham, the man of faith, he entered into a new Covenant with this people, as it were the human race in miniature, jealously (Ex. 20:5) demanded undivided loyalty, and repeatedly sealed this mutual agreement with blood (e.g. Ex. 24:3–8). Through Melchisedech, the mysterious priestly representative of the first cosmic Covenant, the old tradition of natural religion was handed on to Abraham, so that it be fulfilled and transcended (Gen. 14:18–19); for God's designs unfold in unbroken, organic progression. Henceforth, the Israelite people would be "a kingdom of priests, and sacred nation" (Ex. 19:6).

Yahweh now confronted mankind not only in the internal, spiritual experience of his chosen people, and in the "sacraments of nature," but in the "magnalia Dei," the wonderful, miraculous events that erupted into their lives; and in their prophetic and royal leadership, and their provisory religious cult—particularly their Levitical priesthood and their sacrifices that foreshadowed the Christian dispensation. The messianic grace that Yahweh bestowed on them he confirmed in the testimony of external sacramentality, whose signs, though in themselves shadowed sterility, were truly symbolic (Heb. 7:18–19; 5; 10:1). And no longer was he satisfied with anonymous dialogue, but spoke loudly to mankind in inspired revelation—again, it is true, with words replete with enigma that would await clarification in the Messiah himself.

Then, when the fullness of time arrived (Gal. 4:5), the Father, who had formerly overshadowed the Tabernacle of the Old Covenant, now overshadowed Mary, and in holy silence (Wis. 18:14–15) sent his only-begotten Son (1 Jn. 4:9–10), who was born of the Virgin by the same Spirit (Lk. 1:35) who had once moved over the primeval waters (Gn. 1:2). In the immaculate womb of Our Lady the holy marriage of divine and human nature was realized, the incomparable union from whose fertility would emerge new, abundant life for all mankind. In the pure sanctuary of her being, the High Priest, who would offer the absolutely acceptable sacrifice of the New Covenant (Heb. 9:11–14), was consecrated; a new King, who would guide us to victorious salvation, was anointed (Mt. 2:1–3).

This is the "sacredly terrifying mystery" that remains a foolishness and a stumbling-block to so many (1 Cor. 1:23).

The Word was made flesh, and dwelt among us (John 1:14).

"God takes a form, a Name is to be heard; a human being takes among us the place of the Most High" (Karl Barth). "This is, indeed, an unheard-of co-mingling and a paradoxical fusion. He who is, becomes; the Infinite is created and is contained in space . . . The Word becomes reachable by the senses, the Invisible is seen, the Inaccessible is touched, the Timeless steps into time, the Son of God becomes the Son of Man!" (St. Gregory Nazianzen).

Despising shame (Heb. 12:2), the second divine Person took to himself the humiliation, the *kenosis*, of entrance into the concrete, dependent finitude of mankind's reality, with all its contrarieties and grotesqueries, all the misery spawned by sin, excepting sin itself. The First-born (Col. 1:12) plunged with divine earnestness (Wis. 18:14) into the fearful existential condition of estrangement from the Divinity (Phil. 2: 5–8), the tragic plight of his brethren (Heb. 2:17); so that "by the grace of God he might taste death for all" (Heb. 2:9) and destroy its rule (2 Tm. 1:10). He, who had no knowledge of sin, made himself sin, so that we might become God's justice in Him" (2 Cor. 5:21).

Heretofore, God spoke in divers ways and in divers manners to mankind; now he communicates in full, undiluted "I-Thou" dialogue with mankind through his Son (Heb. 1:1), the Prophet, who is himself Truth (Jn. 14:6). And his words, rich and resonant, pierce humanity like a two-edged sword that can penetrate even to the point of division between soul and spirit (Heb. 4:12). Triumphantly, they "shake not the earth only, but heaven also" (Ag. 2:7).

God's primordial sacrament is now the God-Man Himself, the effective sign of divine presence and action. As Father E. Schillebeeckx, O.P., admirably elucidates in *Christ the Sacrament of Encounter with God*, he, who is God in a human way, and man in a divine way, is at once both "the human embodiment of the redeeming love of God" and the supreme realization of man's worship of God. Christ is the unique actualization in human bodiliness (the corporeity that reveals as well as veils human interiority) of God's redeeming, sanctifying power. "Human encounter with Jesus is, therefore, the sacrament of the encounter with God"; and he who is Head of the human race, the New Adam (1 Cor. 15:45), is the prototype of human consecration to God.

Now in the very being of Christ the new, superior Covenant (Heb. 7:23) between the Almighty and mankind, so repeatedly broken by man's infidelity, attains consummate perfection of the divine invitation and of the human response. Christ is the Covenant realized.

This Man-God, "the supreme fulfillment of the Love of the Trinity in such manner that around His Manhood the rest of creation is arranged in time and organized in space; the articulating principle of history and the sun of the universe" (Danielou), opened up God's secrets to man.

With unaffected simplicity, the Gospels tell us that he moved among men and women and children, among the saintly and the sinful; and that he did good (Mk. 7:37). He performed miracles that anticipated the eschatological, divinely energized creation, the new Paradise, that he came to restore.

In his baptism by John (Lk. 3:21–22), the last and greatest witness of the Old Covenant, Christ was consecrated by the Holy Spirit for the beginning of his messianic ministry (Jn. 15:27; Lk. 1:2). Then, exercising his powers as Prophet (Lk. 24:18–19), Priest (Heb. 4:14), and King (Jn. 18:37), he erected the essential structure of his Church, the Kingdom that had been prefigured in the Old Testament, and of which his own earthly life was the advent. He entrusted to its keeping the deposit of faith (Mk. 16:15–16) and sacraments (Jn. 20:22–23; Lk. 22:19–20) whereby all men, his brethren, could be recreated in supernatural life; and he instituted the hierarchical ministry (Mt. 16:18–19; 18:18; Lk. 16:15–16; Jn. 20:23; Lk. 22:19–20; Mt. 5:14, etc.) to bring them both these gifts.

Later, on his departure to heaven, this Church would continue through space and time to be the visible, organic expression, the *societas signum,* of his redeeming grace. His spirit, the other Paraclete (Jn. 14:16–17), would infuse it with life (Acts 2); but first Christ himself, as Messiah, had to win this life in the terrifying mystery of the death that the Father had destined for him (Jn. 7:38–39).

Through the saving worship of his entire life, but particularly through the ineffable, bloody prayer-action of his death on the Cross, the supreme humiliation, our High Priest defeated death and the world (Jn. 16:33), and redeemed fallen mankind. By the universalist character of his sacrifice (graphically symbolized by the wooden beams pointing to North and South, East and West, encompassing "the breadth and length, and height and depth" (Eph. 3:17–19), Christ merited that the human order be recreated (2 Cor. 5:17; Gal. 6:15); that mankind in principle be united with God, the source of supernatural life, and thereby that man be united with man (Eph. 2:13–18). In dying for us (Rom. 5:8) putting sin and death to open shame (Col. 2:14), Christ won all creation—man and the entire cosmos—back into reconciliation with the Creator (Col. 1:19–20). As the first birth out of death (Col. 1:18), he became the vital source of eternal rehabilitation (Heb. 5:9).

Now, it was in Christ's Resurrection that the Father accepted the messianic sacrifice of the One who is both Son of God and Son of Man. Our Lord's glorified humanity was then established as the sign and cause of human redemption and divinization.

But Christ's manhood is no longer earthbound among the dead (Lk. 24:5). Because of the transfiguration of his corporality, immediate bodily encounter between the Savior and us is impossible until the Parousia when we, too, quickened in body as well as in soul by the Holy Spirit, will be completely transferred into the new, supernatural mode of existence.

Consequently, it was expedient (Jn. 16:7) that Our Lord ascend to his Father, not only to intercede for us (Rom. 8:34; Heb. 9:24), but to send the Spirit who, through the sacramental Church, would provide tangible accessibility to Christ's saving power.

The Father, therefore, "bade him sit on his right hand,

above the heavens, high above all princedoms and powers and virtues and dominations, and every name that is known, not in this world only, but in the world to come. He has put everything under his dominion" (Eph. 1:20–22). Christ, who had known utter humiliation, is now exalted exceedingly (Phil. 2:9). He who had, out of love for his Father and for mankind, become a servant (Phil. 2:8), is now invested as Lord, *Kyrios*, King of men and of angels, of all creation (Acts 2:26). The High Priest, who had sacrificed his own self in the bloody immolation of Calvary, now enters in triumph in the eternal Holy of Holies (Heb. 9:11).

Thereby was completed Christ's Pasch, his Passage through death—to resurrection—to ascension, that had been typified through the entire Old Testament, especially in the deliverance of the Chosen People from Egypt into the Promised Land; the Passage in which all mankind is to participate.

He who "has gone up, high above the heavens, to fill creation with his presence" (Eph. 4:10), has gone to prepare for us, his brethren. Having led captivity captive, he is anxious to send gifts to mankind (Eph. 4:8). He who had been lifted up on the infamous gibbet, is now lifted up above creation to draw us, and in us the entire universe, by a mysterious gravitation to himself in the realm of the Trinity. The Divine Bridegroom has entered into his Father's house to celebrate there an eternal union with his Bride, redeemed humanity. The slain Lamb comes to open the book in which are inscribed the names of the elect (Ap. 5:2–6).

Christ's earthly mission has been completed (Heb. 1:3). *Thus, "exalted at God's right hand, he claims from his Father his promise to bestow the Holy Spirit"* (Acts 2:31). And so begins the work of the Third Person, to whom Christ has entrusted all that he had merited for us (Jn. 16:14–15). It is this Paraclete who will henceforth impart salvation to all Christ's brethren, interiorly and personally.

Again, as preceded the first creation, that of the cosmos, and the second creation, that of the Humanity of Christ, a holy silence surrounded not only earth, but heaven (Ap. 8:1).

And "when the fifty days were accomplished" (meaning the fullness of the Pasch, for fifty, according to ancient symbolism, signifies superplenitude), the followers of the Lord "were all together in one place. And suddenly there came a sound from heaven, as of a violent wind blowing, and it filled the whole house where they were sitting. And there appeared to them what seemed to be tongues of fire, which parted and came to rest on each of them; and they were all filled with the Holy Spirit, and began to speak in strange tongues, as the Spirit gave utterance to each. Among those who were dwelling in Jerusalem at this time were devout Jews from every country under heaven; so, when the noise of this went abroad, the crowd which gathered was in bewilderment; each man severally heard them speak in his own language. And they were all beside themselves with astonishment. 'Are not they all Galileans speaking,' they asked. 'How is it that each of us hears them talking his own native tongue? There are Parthians among us and Medes and Elamites; our homes are in Mesopotamia, or Judea or Cappadocia; in Pontus or Asis, Phrygia or Pamphlia, Egypt or the parts of Libya round Cyrene; some of us are Jews and others proselytes; there are Cretans among us, too, and Arabians; and each has been hearing them tell of God's wonders in his own language.' So they were all beside themselves with perplexity, and asked one another, 'What can this mean?' There were others who said, mockingly, 'They have had their fill of new wine.'

"But Peter, with eleven apostles at his side, stood there and raised his voice to speak to them: 'Men of Judea," he said, 'and all of you who are dwelling in Jerusalem, I must tell you this; listen to what I have to say. These men are not drunk, as you suppose; it is only the third hour of the day. This is what was foretold by the prophet, Joel: In the last times, God says, I will pour out my spirit upon all mankind, and your sons and daughters will be prophets. Your young men shall see visions, and your old men shall dream dreams; and I will pour out my Spirit in these days upon my servants and handmaids, so that they will prophesy' " (Acts 2:1–8).

And so took place the event of the First Pentecost, the crown of the Paschal mystery (St. Augustine), the consummation of the "great Sunday," Christ's Death-Resurrection-Ascension (St. Athanasius). This is "the metropolis, the capital of the feasts" that spans the great space between Our Lord's departure and his return on the last day.

It is the emergence of the "Eighth Day" of creation, as the Epistle of Barnabas expresses it; for it is the formal inauguration of a new existence, wherein "all things are made new" (2 Cor. 5:17). It is the awakening of a new, transfigured humanity.

In the first creation the Spirit of God brooded over what was to be (Gen. 1:2); and then "God formed man of the slime of the earth, and breathed into his face the breath of life, and man became a living soul" (Gen. 2:7). Now, the Church, already established in its radical structure and operation by Christ, is animated by a supernatural breathing by the Holy Spirit for the life, not of this world, but of heaven (1 Cor. 15:45); and the living, Mystical Body of Christ, the New Adam (1 Cor. 15:45) enters history, gradually, determinedly, bringing its content into the depth and height and length and breadth of his Paschal mystery.

6 * Christ's Church

> *When I talk about the Church, I cannot stop!*
>
> St. Augustine
>
> *The Mystical Head, which is Christ, and the Church which here below as another Christ shows forth His Person, constitute one new Man in whom heaven and earth are joined together in perpetuating the work of the Cross: Christ, we mean, the Head and the Body, the Whole Christ.*
>
> Pope Pius XII—Mystici Corporis
>
> *Why, Jesus and the Church, it is all one!*
>
> St. Joan of Arc

THE CATHOLIC CHURCH, the "mystery hidden from eternity" (Eph. 3:9), is the gathering place of all the mysteries of our Faith: of the Triune God revealing himself to mankind, of the wonder of the Word's Incarnation, of the whole complex work of the Redemption.

Consequently, the Church may be viewed from innumerable different aspects, all complementary, each one focusing on yet another characteristic of the Church's extraordinary composition.

We have referred to its reality as the Mystical Body of the New Adam, Christ, a theme that we will return to momentarily. But we must bear in mind that we may also rewardingly consider the Church as the Bride of Christ (Eph. 5:23–33; Ap. 19:6–9); as the Kingdom of Heaven on earth (Eph. 5:5; Ap. 1:6); as the City that is one in fellowship" (Ps. 121:3); as the "new universe" (St. Gregory of Nyssa), for which all the cosmos was created (Hermas); as God's Vineyard (Jn. 15:1–11; Lk. 20:9–19) and Vine (Jn. 15:1–17; Cor. 3:6–9); as the

51

"people of the new inheritance" (Epistle of Barnabas), "God's Israel" (Gal. 8:16), "made up of every nation, tribe, people and language" (Ap. 7:9); as the "great "Sacrament of Christ" (St. Augustine); the "people of God" (1 Ptr. 2:10). All these expressions, "although they do not cohere organically into a logical whole, complete, correct, and balance one another; and thus they all join together to give us, not an exhaustive idea of the Church—which could not be—but a knowledge which is adapted to our condition" (Henri de Lubac).

It is particularly as a visible, ecclesiastical society that Christ's Church presents itself to the world at large. Frequently this institutional aspect of the Church is all too human—excessively so, remarks Hans Küng—such that even its human reality, let alone its divine, becomes a stumbling block and a rock of offense to many (Rom. 9:33). However, this shattering fallibility is a constitutive element in the Church's actual make-up, a profound continuation of the incarnative mystery within the divine economy of Redemption. As the sacred Humanity of the Son of Man was disfigured by his brethren so that he had to be labeled "man" (Jn. 19:5), the human part of the Church continues to be defiled by the sin of its members.

Be that as it may, even Catholics often fail to realize that "though the Church is a hierarchical society, it is so in a different way from the various societies of which we have actual experience in our daily lives" (Msgr. André Pailler). Its visible, human structure and function is touched by the energies of the Holy Spirit, and are only analogously similar to those of other societies. Failing to appreciate this truth, our concept of the Church remains false, a sort of Cartesian clear and distinct idea that never leaves the natural plane.

Nor is this all. Henri de Lubac cautions us that in struggles against heresy the Catholic apologist "always sees the question, more or less willingly or unwillingly, from the heretic's point of view, often accepting questions in the form the heretic propounds them; so that, whilst not sharing the error, he often makes implicit concessions to his opponent that are more serious the more explicit his refutation. . . . Heresy may be the occasion of a progress that may be one-sided, and the occasion in turn of further error." This is a danger that, unfortunately, has been well illustrated in the history of the idea of the Church in the average Christian consciousness. The Pauline-patristic concept of the Church was that of a Church not merely hierarchical, but also and essentially the Mystical Body of Christ, vivified by the Holy Spirit. This integral concept prevailed until the barbarian invasions in Europe, when the enormous influx of unlettered converts necessitated far-reaching initiative and direction from clerics. Exaggerated dependence on clerical action not infrequently engendered and even encouraged passivity on the part of the laity, and developed the tendency to identify in practice the Church with its institutional form of external authority.

With the emergence of the Caesaro-papist threat, especially as evidenced in the turbulent investiture controversy and later in the Gallican doctrines, the Church rigidly and militantly defended its juridical character against the encroachments of secular society. This one-sided emphasis of the hierarchical-canonical aspect of the Church was further disastrously intensified in Catholic apologetic after the Protestant revolt, and still more during the deistic Enlightenment when naturalism influenced even ecclesiological studies. By then even the parish, the *ecclesia* here-and-now, was widely regarded in practice as primarily a geographical, organizational entity, little more.

But the inevitable reaction has set in. Today the average Catholic consciousness is beginning to penetrate beyond mere circumscribed, legal concepts to the re-thinking and realization of the Church as a universal community in faith, worship and love; the organic Mystical Body of Christ. As Guardini remarked a half century ago, "The Church has awakened in our souls!"

This awakening, it must be admitted, is sometimes not without mishap; for within the exuberant rejection of centralized absolutism and the new "discovery" of the Church, there lurks the temptation to reply against one extreme with another—in the present instance by belittling and reducing to a minimum the importance of the juridical Church, that of "ruler and subject, authority and obedience, human legislators and human laws, the Church of external, visible and human elements." The piddling, impetuous, platonizing mentality behind such repudiation fails to recognize, for example, that "the purpose of all ecclesiastical jurisdiction, even that which tends immediately to the external good, ultimately is reduced to this, the better attainment of the interior sanctification of the faithful, and through it their eternal happiness" (Michiels). Instead it holds in contemptuous suspicion all the juridical-social order, especially its legalistic apparatus, and feeds, with feverish zeal, on blurred mystique. Its final orientation, even though unintentional, is actually directed towards the denial of the "paradoxical logic" of the incarnational mystery in God's economy of Redemption.

Notwithstanding, the heartening fact remains that the average Catholic consciousness is becoming increasingly aware of the full dimensions to the essential nature of the Catholic Church, acknowledging with Pope Pius XII (in his encyclical *Mystici Corporis*) that "to describe the Church of Christ—

which is the Holy, Catholic, Apostolic, Roman Church—there is no name more noble, none more divine, than the Mystical Body of Christ."

. . . . *And the new, living Body of Christ, the Mystical Adam, enters history.*

Scripture tells us that Christ "must have his dwelling-place in heaven, until the time when all is restored anew" (Acts 3:21); that is, he remains in relative absence until his Body is built up to perfect stature (Eph. 3:21).

For, whilst the Church that he founded during his lifetime on earth is a society whose structure is shaped by the threefold deposit of faith, sacraments, and apostolic powers (that bring both of the latter gifts to mankind), its essential nature reaches into infinitely more profound dimensions. It is not just a social aggregate. Astoundingly, the Catholic Church is "his Body, the completion of him who fills the members with all graces" (Eph. 1:23); and "He is the Head of the Church, his Body, of which he is the Savior" (Eph. 5:23).

"A head and a body go to make one man," comments St. Augustine, "and Christ and his Church combine to make one Man, a perfect Man." In like manner Bossuet: "The Church is Jesus Christ diffused and communicated; Jesus Christ whole; Jesus Christ perfect Man; Jesus Christ in his fullness."

The modern Anglican writer, D. L. Mackinnon, unhesitatingly declares that "we cannot understand the Church if we have misunderstood the Christ. Conversely, we may make bold to say that an understanding of Christ necessarily entails an understanding of the Church." And de Lubac, elucidating the thought of Origen, continues further: "For a body Christ has not only the individual flesh which John bears witness that he saw and touched. His taking of the individual flesh has, of course, a unique importance as being the point of insertion of

God into our humanity. But it was not an end in itself: its purpose is to make possible the taking to himself the Church. Hence this Body which is the Church . . . must, in Origen's way of speaking, be 'truer' than the body of the individual flesh, because it constitutes a more perfect, a 'fuller' realization of the divine plan. It is the end; the body of the flesh was the means. It is the reality, of which the flesh, even in its reality, is the 'type,' the symbol. The historic life of the Savior symbolizes a vaster life, that of his 'true and perfect body.' 'The body of Jesus,' says Origen, 'seems to be a figure of the Church.' "

The glorified, physical Christ is, of course, transcended to his Body the Church; but is most definitely his Body in a very real sense—"mystical" as the theological precision subtly puts it, distinguishing the Church from the physical body of Christ, and from mere moral organizations.

In the divine economy Christ *needs* a "mystical" body.

Writes E. Schillebeeckx, O.P.: "It is as man that the Son is the mediator of grace; he is mediator in his Humanity, according to the ways of humanity. His human mediation of grace, therefore, presupposes his corporeality."

In other words, the Incarnation continues; the Son of God retains the human nature, in all its ramifications, that he had assumed. But Christ's human bodiliness is now transfigured in glory, whilst we remain earthbound, and therefore unable to encounter him in full human mode. And we need his visible, human availability. We need to touch him if we are to receive a communication of his grace (Jn. 20:19–31). This, precisely, is what we are enabled to do through his Church, the earthly extension of his human corporeality, his redeeming Incarnation continued in time and space, the great Sacrament into which all that was visible in Christ has now passed (St. Leo the Great).

Moreover, absolutely speaking it is only the God-Man who may enter heaven (Jn. 3:12). But by mystically recapitulating all mankind in his glorified Humanity through his Church, his complement, he can summon all into his most intimate presence (Eph. 5:27), and become the living door whereby mankind gains access to the Divinity (Jn. 1:1). He alone is the Alpha; but through his Mystical Body he, and redeemed mankind in him, constitute the Omega (Ap. 1:8; 22:6; 22:13).

And so, he who is "the beginning, the firstborn from the dead" (Col. 1:18–19), has become the One of whose fulness mankind receives (Jn. 1:16). He is the spring that overflows with the water of life (Ap. 22:1), the fire that sears with purifying, creative flame (Lk. 12:49), the leaven that permeates and transforms (Mt. 13:33–35). By the power of his Spirit, the New Paraclete, the superabundant grace that was once contained in his Manhood is now poured out on mankind through his Church, literally transfiguring it from within its depths, such that the Church is the marrow and matrix of a new humanity in Christ. And this communication of supernatural life to his Church is so uniquely profound, that the inspired work of Scripture does not hesitate to compare it analogously with the vital relationship that exists between a living man's head and his body.

It is humanity, and through humanity all the "elements of the world," that provides Christ with the material, the "flesh" —the concrete, changing, diversity of the human make-up— for his Mystical Body. By the ineffable workings of the Holy Spirit, through the Church, and in the spirit and pattern of Mary, the world continues to offer era by era, place by place, culture by culture, a new Body for the Word of God to assume. And through its tangible reality Christ, in his Paschal mystery, continues to be made sacramentally present, by an "ascending incarnation," in different places and in successive times. His Spirit permeates into the furthest reaches of mankind, purifying and transfiguring it from within, creating a new humanity.

Here, then is the magnificent design of God in the messianic interval between Christ's Ascension and his return: the building up (Mt. 16:18) of the Mystical Body, the Church, "to the mature measure of the fullness of Christ" (Eph. 4:13) —the complete vital participation of faithful mankind in the Paschal mystery of the Kyrios.

This awesome work will be accomplished by the joint action of the Holy Spirit, in a mission that is at once distinct (Gal. 4:4–6) and homogeneous with that of Christ in purpose and consent, and the ecclesiastical institution of the Church, in an actual sharing of Christ's own mission (Jn. 17:16–18, 22–23).

The apostolate of the Church—the hierarchic ministry of Word, sacrament and spiritual governance, and the witnessing, the "doing in charity" (Eph. 4:15) of all its members—is specifically the result and continuation of Christ's own messianic mission of love (Jn. 17:16–18). This apostolate will be our concern further on. For the present, let it suffice to re-emphasize that its movement is towards the restoration, unification and transformation of all mankind, and through man the entire range of the universe, in Christ unto God: the building up of his "communional" Body.

But this apostolate of the institutional Church, the visible pledge and actual expression of the active presence of Christ and his redemptive grace, is, in its innermost depths, the "ministry of the Spirit" (2 Cor. 3:18). The Church is, in fact, "the society of the Spirit" (St. Augustine). It is not only Christocentric, in that our Lord is its Head and its very existence is the fullness of his life, it is also Spirit-centered, for it is dynamically unified in and by the Holy Spirit. As the encyclical *Mystici Corporis* reiterated with unmistakable emphasis, the Church is indwelt by the Third Person of the Blessed Trinity, who is truly its soul, the quickening principle that animates into movement and fruitfulness its total organism.

Obviously, the Holy Spirit is not the soul of the Church in the same manner that our souls inform our bodies. There is no physical, substantial union involved, but rather a union of alliance (Mt. 28:20). We must remember that the nature of the Church is revealed not only by its mysterious dependency as his Bride (Ap. 19:6–9). It is a distinct, subsisting entity. Sent by Christ (Jn. 15:16) and receiving of Christ (16:15), the Holy Spirit, therefore, indwells (1 Cor. 3:16–17; 6:19) the Body already constituted in being by Christ during his lifetime on earth.

It is the Holy Spirit who moves to fulfillment the redemptive plan begun in embryonic form by the Word-made-Flesh, in obedience to his Father. Otherwise it would remain static, barren (Ez. 38). Always acting in relation to Christ's work, he applies individually and collectively, the graces won by our Savior (Jn. 16:14–15). Within the hidden depths of man's being (Gal. 4:6), he is the vital law that regulates the growth of the Church in unity (Acts 4:32; 9:31; 1 Cor. 1:10).

He effects interiorly what the apostolate of the institutional Church effects in the external order of the economy of salvation established by Christ.

It is he who appoints Christ's apostles (Mk. 1:8) and impels them forward on their mission (Acts 20:28). Abiding within them (Jn. 14:16–17) this divine Teacher recreates them interiorly (2 Cor. 5:17; Gal. 4:6–7), gradually transforming them in the likeness of Christ by infusing into them the very life of God (Rom. 5:5). He distributes among them the manifold complementary gifts (1 Cor. 12:6–11; Eph. 4:11;

Rom. 12:4), whereby, according to their different functions, they continue and perfect (Jn. 14:12) Christ's messianic work.

By his fecundating power the Church's apostles are made men of truth (Acts 2:4; 4:12; 1 Pt. 1:12); and he prepares their listeners for the fruitful reception of the Word (1 Cor. 12:3).

He gives intrinsic potency to the Church's sacraments (Mk. 1:8; Jn. 20:22–23). By the communication of his power (1 Cor. 12:13) all who are baptized out of water by the Church are not only made "members of the household of God, and fellow citizens of the saints" (Eph. 2:19), but are in such "concorporation" with others by reason of their incorporation into the Mystical Body of Christ (1 Cor. 12:13)—a union so intimate that they are "placed in symbiosis" with our Lord, as Yves Congar strikingly expressed it, and live by the divine life (Phil. 1:22; Gal. 11:20).

Moreover, while soul of the Church, "effecting interiorly what the hierarchic ministry effects exteriorly," the Holy Spirit remains transcendent to the Mystical Body of Christ; and in this extraordinary freedom he further builds up the Church by unpredictable interventions into human history, individual and collective, and the bestowal of additional graces.

Thus the Church, the Mystical Body of Christ, the New Adam, advances through time and space by the joint activity of the Holy Spirit and the ecclesial apostolate. Unremittingly it labors to unite, through Christ, the whole of mankind, with the Triune God, thus forming the individual man into an integrity within his innermost being—an integrity infinitely open to truth and love; and thereby also bringing all men, now brothers in Christ, into communion with each other. Its ultimate goal is the Return of the glorified Lord when, its sacramental signs no longer required, and its predestined stature attained, all will be made new (2 Ptr. 3:13), and God will be all in all (Eph. 1:23). The New Adam, in his victorious plenitude, will burst asunder that cramped dimensions of time-space duration and enter into the full expanse of eternal glory.

7 ✳ The Church Today

> Our period has decided for a secular world.
>
> Paul Tillich

> We should have a great love for our age, but make no concession to the spirit of the age, so that in us the Christian mystery may never lose its sap.
>
> Henri de Lubac, S.J.

> Let the world know this: the Church looks at the world with profound understanding, with sincere admiration, and with sincere intention, not of conquering it but of serving it, not of despising it but of appreciating it, not of condemning it but of strengthening and saving it.
>
> Pope Paul VI

Someone has remarked, no doubt, cynically, that for the foreseeable future statistics will decidedly not favor the Church.

To comprehend the significance of this observation, we need only recall that, while more than seventy percent of the world human population live on the continents of Asia and Africa and in Oceania, they have only ten percent of the Catholic Church's total membership. The remaining ninety percent live in Europe and in the North and South Americas.

We have already noted the fantastic growth in world population in recent times. The disquieting fact is that there is no proportionate increase in Christian people. For instance, it is estimated that between 1883 and 1956 the population of Asia and Indonesia increased by 640 million persons, whereas the number of Catholics gained by only 23 million. For the same period, the statistics for Africa were 120 million increase of total population, with 18 million growth of Church membership; for Oceania, 10 million advance of total population included a two and one-half million increase of Catholic population—the same proportion, one fourth, as in Europe. And, finally, in America, while the total growth was 250 million, 142 million were Catholics—by far the most spectacular numerical extension of the Church in our time.

Statistics definitely indicate important aspects of the situation of Christ's Mystical Body in our contemporary world. To ignore them would be folly. Their value should be reckoned with prudently, and then be complemented by evaluation that goes beyond mere numbers.

The Catholic Church of our era exists in a condition of "diaspora." It is a dispersed minority, a "stranger" to the contemporary world in the sense of the word used by St. Peter in his first Epistle (2:11).

No longer is it the Church of an enclosed, homogeneous, more or less stationary civilization of medieval "Christendom." With the expansion of the West into the full dimensions of global history, the Church not only won to its membership peoples of all nations, it became a minority within a pluralistic human society. This was due to many reasons, capital among them being not only the nature of the Church itself as a stumbling block and contradiction to humanity (1 Cor. 1:23), but the widespread apostasy of Western man, and his failure in most cases to implant the Mystical Body of Christ in the vast new regions of the earth that he indefatigably brought under his influence.

Sociologically, as Rahner rightly observes, the Church has taken on the character of a sect, one religious organization among others. During these recent centuries it has experienced profound sloughing-offs, conditioned by rapid agitations that criss-crossed modern history. Its enormous influence and control over public life, as obtained in medieval Christendom, has been abandoned, not infrequently by force—a stripping of temporal power that has manifestly benefited the spiritual caliber of the Church, and, other factors aside, that contributed to the maturity of secular society in its many valid autonomies.

The world in which it exists today is no longer "Constantinian," replete with institutions that provide favorable climate and sub-structures for its development, and even a juridical status for its clerical representatives. It is not a "sacral" society, as Maritain expressed it. Most of its institutions are completely divorced from all organized religion, and quite often militate against Christian beliefs and practices; and this obtains even though, ironically, many non-Western peoples continue to associate Christianity with their "arch-aggressor" the West, an identification that constitutes one of the greatest obstacles to the evangelization of millions.

Rahner, among others, reminds us that we should consider the contemporary "diaspora" one of those mysterious "musts" in the economy of Salvation (Mt. 16:23), all fundamentally the shadow of mankind's murder of Christ.

The present diaspora ought not to be, for its origin in human guilt remains condemned. But in the overwhelming proportions of its actual, historical concreteness, it appears as another mysterious move in the Divine Plan wherein the Holy Spirit, who does not will man's fault, can nevertheless infallibly draw good out of the effects of his fault. It is part of the darkness that the Easter hymn, *Exultet*, declares blessed: *O vere beata nox!*

Consequently, it is a time when Christians must combine heroically zealous missionary activity with calm, Christlike composure; when they must adjust their interior life and apostolate to the conditions of the diaspora—never by way of compromise, but always by way of the vital, purifying, assimilative adaptation of the divine-human organism of Christ's Mystical Body to the space-time complex in which it develops.

Inevitably, there are those Catholics who (often with militant fanaticism) would have the Church entrench itself in a theocratic ghetto, a closed circle of the elect, safeguarded from a world that is irrevocably evil—a condition for which the Catholic can bear no responsibility whatsoever. They would have us play safe, apparently impervious to the sad, stinging indictments of "outsiders" such as Camus ("There can be cause for shame being happy all alone.") and Gide ("Why do Catholics have such a bite?"). For these egocentrics the Church is no "movement, a force in motion," as Bernanos puts it, "but only a shelter, a kind of spiritual inn through whose windows one can enjoy watching the passers-by, the people on the outside, who do not dwell in the inn, trudging through the mud. . . ."

And there are also the many (whose scandal we consider elsewhere) who are utterly and shockingly indifferent to their brethren both within the Church and outside it. Theirs is the abysmal travesty of Christianity that incited Kierkegaard to hurl his scorn against the "church of nincompoops."

But neither the advocates of an anachronistic ghetto policy, nor the many who decide for an enfeebled, emasculated Catholicism, can hide the extraordinary awakening of intrepid missionary spirit among contemporary Catholics. They may be bishops, priests, religious, members of Secular Institutes, Catholic Actionists; they may be missionaries in the full, traditional sense of the word, sent to establish the visible Church in new regions; or "missionaries of the interior," as Cardinal Cardijn called them, bent on restoring to Christ milieux—people and institutions—that were once Christian. They may be contemplatives like Therese of Lisieux, Patroness of the Missions. *They all profoundly realize that the Church and mission are inseparable.*

Faithful to Christ in his Church, they are fully aware of individual persons' actual preference of darkness to the light of God, and the evil of their works (Jn. 3:19): they are not deliberately blind sentimentalists. But, convinced of the "Christic" greatness of all men, they realize that very much of what is done by those outside the society of the Church is "performed in God" (Jn 3:21), even if in its unsuspected, hidden depths.

They admit, in sturdy humility, that "much of the hatred and the scorn which many powerful minds have displayed in our time toward Catholicism, is the product of a love betrayed: it is the defense and the rebellion of a man who has been wounded" (M. D. Chenu); that countless persons have been alienated from Christ's Church by the "evasive tone, the words and indiscriminately proffered obsequiousities, the suavities and ambiguities of spiritual gesture, the clever knowledge of unseen allusion, and the equivocal ellipses which disfigure the Christian witness of our times" (Emmanuel Mounier).

While painfully conscious of the distance (more spiritual than physical) that separates present-day Catholicism from the contemporary world, these missionary Catholics are buoyed up by an unremitting hope, not only by reason of the

Christian triumph that is already theirs in principle, but because of the enormous existing opportunities for mutual encounter between the Church, through themselves, and today's "outside," "Neighborhood," world.

They are convinced, for example, that today's climate of despair is never wholly foreign to authentic religious anguish, and that within the present promethean scientism there emerges an exciting opportunity to prove that contemporary man may "steal" fire from heaven and still recognize Almighty God. They submit that "the presence of God in modern society necessarily demands a modality which will be new" (Gustave Weigel).

They are willing, with an audacity obedient to the directives of the Holy Spirit in the hierarchical Church, to enter into a living, active dialogue with the "others" of today's neo-pagan cosmos, even with those whom Schleiermacher called the Church's "Cultured Despisers"—a dialogue, not only of words (real words, not forbidding jargon) but of action; one of bold prudence, critical charity, patient anxiety, and humble confidence, a dynamic expression of Christian universalism.

Actually, this "Dialogue of Salvation" (Pope Paul VI) that demands their total commitment is not limited to that with non-believers. Its dimensions are many. To fulfill their duty as Catholics in a world that will demand fresh, unprecedented application of eternal principles, it has been necessary for them to take stock of their own condition, and to "rediscover" the vast reality of the Church in all its purity, stripped of so many anachronistic encumbrances erected by human customs.

Consequently, contemporary Catholics, through prayer and study individually and collectively, are engaged in the absolutely requisite dialogue with the Holy Spirit, the One who alone can bring to light the many-splendored reality of the Mystical Body of Christ, and guide them through the labyrinth of dangers that threaten their zeal. We may expect in the imminent unfolding of our era a new impetus in studies relative to the activity of the Holy Spirit in the history of salvation.

They are involved in the dialogue between priest and layman. Recent centuries have witnessed a scandalous separation of clerics and laity, a state of affairs that must be corrected if the Church's mission is to be fully effective. For, as Cardinal Suhard never failed to emphasize, "the complete evangelist is not just the baptized Christian, nor the priest by himself, it is the Christian community. The basic cell, the unit of measurement in the apostolate, is a kind of organic composite, the inseparable pair—priest and laity." In our time, fortunately, a rapport between the two is being forged (inevitably in much spiritual suffering), avoiding the evils of the two extremes, clericalism and laicism.

Furthermore, there is developing, with singular enthusiasm, the dialogue between Catholics and their separated baptized brethren—members of the Orthodox and Protestant Churches, who number half of the world Christian population. The alert twentieth-century Catholics are ecumenists who pray and work for the reunification of sundered Christianity. The desire of Christ that all may be one in charity (Jn. 17:11) presses them to apply themselves, in this century of "total" warfare, to the holy task of peace between the brethren of Jesus of Nazareth.

They are profoundly aware of the presence of "anonymous" Catholics in the milieux in which they move; persons who do not publicly belong to the Church, but who are activated by supernatural grace, and whom the Holy Spirit pits, as it were, in competition against his Church, ever anxious that they emulate in sanctity.

There is also the activated dialogue between contemporary Catholics and the people whom God has marked with his special blessing. They mystery of Israel haunts those members of the Messiah's Mystical Body who are truly sensitive to the spiritual currents that pervade our era—one that is already drenched in the blood of millions of immolated Jews. While themselves awaiting the Return of their Lord, these Catholics seek to enter into authentic "I-Thou" relationship (as Buber would express it) with those who still await his first coming.

And there is the delicate, laborious dialogue between Catholics and the peoples of "pre-Christian" paganism. Probably nowhere has this contemporary dialogue been more graphically exemplified than in the actual life of Father Charles de Foucald, "brother of the Touaregs," who, with Christian empathy, endeavored as best he could to enter into the total human (including the religious) mentality of this people. Essentially, it involves the enormous effort of making Christianity redemptively incarnate in all that is good—and there is much!—in the religious intuitions and modes of spirituality of these paganisms; as it were, to help bring about new epiphanies of Christ the Savior from within the very texture of purified non-Christian religious cultures.

In many instances here—as in the Catholic's engagement with the neo-pagan milieux—the dialogue is "pre-missionary" (Fr. Peyriguère), one of presence, prayer and sacrifice before talk. In this situation the Catholic apostle becomes heroically a veritable dialogue in himself, being at once a "messenger of the Christ who cannot yet give his Name," and a "representative of those who do not believe, do not pray." The need for such a dialogue of presence is becoming more and more widespread in our contemporary world.

At the hub of this many-faceted dialogue of the Church unfolds the Second Vatican Council.

Its goal, as outlined by Pope John XXIII in his encyclical *Ad Petri Cathedram*, consists in "promoting the development of the Catholic faith, the moral renewal of the Christian life in the faithful, the adaptation of ecclesiastical discipline to the needs and methods of our time."

To what extent it meets this threefold pressing need remains to be seen. Because of the human failings involved, it is unquestionably possible that the Council not have the interior success that the conditions of the contemporary Church, the whole of Christendom, and all humanity demand. The catastrophic failure of the Fifth Council of Lateran (1512–17) is a tragic reminder of this possibility.

But emerging from the progressive-reactionary tension and clash within the Council (representative of the organic "dialectic" within the universal Church) are many indications that the Council is most assuredly moving in the direction of the honest, courageous *aggiornamento* that was boldly requested by Pope John XXIII. Its pastoral-liturgical-ecumenical thrust ("Through renewal of the Catholic Church to reunion of separated Christians"), tuned to the here-and-now of history, is manifest in such different aspects of the Council as its dramatic move to activate the local churches through the reemphasis of the episcopal college, and its widespread, matter-of-fact interpenetration by the biblical spirit. All this is deeply encouraging.

"Only one thing can give real success to any council, and in a very special way to this Council," writes Hans Küng. "Neither some sort of opportunistic 'modernization,' nor some sort of traditionalistic 'restoration,' but only a radical theological and practical concentration—proceeding *from* our own times, and *for* our own times, in the Holy Spirit—on the Gospel of our Lord, Jesus Christ."

Optimistic illusion aside, the Second Vatican Council already provides solid reason to look hopefully for its creative leadership throughout the years and centuries ahead.

8 ✳ The Christian People

> *The complete evangelist is not just the baptized Christian, nor the priest by himself; it is the Christian community. The basic cell, the unit of measurement in the apostolate, is a kind of organic composite, the inseparable pair—priest and laity.*
>
> Cardinal Suhard

> *Those who love his Coming.*
>
> (2 Tm. 4:8)

> *In this world the Church is a mixed community, and will stay like that to the very end—unthreshed corn, the ark with both clean and unclean animals, a ship full of unruly passengers who always seem to be on the point of wrecking it.*
>
> Henri de Lubac, S.J.

THE CATHOLIC CHURCH incarnates Christ's victorious, redeeming grace in space-time duration, so that, in its existence and operation, it is Christ mystically present and acting in the concrete, human context. It is his Pasch historically continued, made an abiding, visible societal event in its essential mystery.

Consequently, all who are baptized into the incarnational

organism of the Church and become, as St. Peter Damian put it, each one the "Church in miniature"—are not only drawn into a concorporation by supernatural faith, hope and charity with the rest of the Christian community (wherein their spiritual individuality, now intensified and elevated pneumatically by the Holy Spirit, find fruition), but are so by reason of their incorporation into Christ himself. For they are truly, mystically united with him in his Paschal Mystery, in his death and in his resurrection (Col. 3:3; Rom. 6:5–11). The outpourings of the Holy Spirit that were inaugurated by Christ's Resurrection (Acts 2:17–21) have already begun their work of spiritualization, transforming those baptized from being "outer men," closed and opaque in the death of sin, into "inward men," open and vibrant in the life of the triumphant Lord (Eph. 3:16; 2 Cor. 4:16; 5:5).

Moreover, in their personal ecclesial status and empowerment as the "Church in miniature," Christians are "commissioned, by their very nature, to be bearers of the function of the Church, as the visible and social manifestation of grace, and to do so by a personal decision to take up, accept, and realize this manifestation in their whole life" (Karl Rahner). Through the sacramental presence and action of their everyday existence theirs is the grandeur to make present and manifest the Church (and therefore Christ) as a tangible "event" in the definite historicity in which they find themselves, so that Christ can encounter all men in their being as free, corporal and historical persons.

Well, then, all who are baptized into Christ are inserted into his Priesthood; for Christ is Priest by nature, having been ordained in the sanctuary of Mary's womb by the power of the Paraclete: His very Name and "priest" are interchangeable terms.

To all his people he communicates, through his Spirit, the

Deifier, a real, analogical sharing in his Priestly powers, en-
abling them to offer divine worship in an acceptable manner
by active participation in his own infinite act of Sacrifice. He
actually anoints them, the chosen members of his Mystical
Body, a priestly people (Exod. 8:6; Is. 61:6; 1 Pt. 2:5–9), investing all of them with an unutterable dignity, and entrusting
them with awesome responsibility. "All are priests," St.
Augustine says simply, "by virtue of the fact that they are
members of Christ;" for through the deliberate, humble, confident union of their daily prayer and offerings—their "spiritual service" (Rom. 12:1–2)—with the supreme Sacrifice of
the Savior, they prolong his priestly holocaust in tangible history, making their whole lives a cult of homage, of glory and
gratitude (Ps. 104:1–5) to the Almighty God.

Christ is also Prophet (Lk. 24:18–19), who was anointed
for his prophetic ministry—the preaching of the inscrutable
mysteries of God to the poor (Lk. 4:16–21)—by the Holy
Spirit in his baptism by John (Mk. 1:9–11). He is Prophet,
supreme witness to the Truth (Jn. 18:37), by his very nature,
for he himself is the Truth (14:6) the Word-made-flesh
(1:14). To his people, purchased by the witness of his very
blood, he has entrusted his gospel, bidding them to honor his
Father by witnessing to its sacred content (Rom. 1:9). Rescued by his sacrifice from darkness into light (1 Pt. 2:9), they
must become, like him, the light of the world (Mt. 5, 14–16),
which will remain plunged in darkness without their help
(Rom. 10:14).

Public testimony to his Word must, therefore, be their
daily, pressing anxiety (1 Cor. 11:28–29), urgent in season and
out of season (2 Tm. 4:2–4).

It may not be confined to a mere proclamation by word (often petulant jargon, religious bromide), but must be lived in

the entire fabric of their lives (Rom. 1:9). It must be prac-
ticed in love (Eph. 4:15), never oriented by brash, imprudent
proselytism that fails to respect the sacredness of human
liberty.

Nor may it ever be jeopardized by dependence on the
propagandistic methods of men, but must lean on the power
of God (1 Cor. 2:1–5). Worthy means are to be employed in
the dissemination of God's message: this goes without saying;
but Christ's people must remember that it is God who appeals
through them, not human wisdom, no matter how persuasive
(2 Cor. 5:20; 1 Cor. 1:17–25; 2:1–16). The Gospel is not
theirs, but of God (Jn. 7:16). This truth forgotten, their witness becomes the absurdity of sounding brass, tinkling symbol,
blaring loudspeaker (1 Cor. 13:1). For their task is not to
please the oscillating whims of men (2 Tm. 4:2–4; Gal. 1:10)
by glibly perverting or abridging the Gospel (Gal. 1:6–8), but
rather by sharing it in all its disturbing purity (2 Cor. 2:17).

And Christ is King (Jn. 18:37), King of the ages (1 Tm.
1:17), King of Kings (1 Tm. 6:16). For as Head (Eph.
1:22–23) and Savior (Col. 1:18–20) of all mankind, and
through mankind of the entire universe, he has executive,
judiciary and legislative power over all creation.

Through baptism he communicates a true participation in
his Kingship to his people, elevating them (who are already,
by their natural, human destiny, rulers of the cosmos) to a divine dignity, and investing them with divine prerogatives.
They are truly a royal people (1 Pt. 2:9), their universal community a kingdom (Ex. 19:5–6).

As such their duty and privilege is to re-establish all created
being (sundered and estranged from its source by man's sin)
in Christ (Eph. 1:10), spiritualizing, unifying, humanizing, redeeming and consecrating the entire universe for the divine

glory (1 Cor. 10:31). This task of overwhelming grandeur they must accomplish through the multiple channels of the duties of their states of life, thereby becoming "agents of Christian renewal."

Now, in order that the members of the Church, his Mystical Body, may be able to fulfill their threefold mission, as sharers in his Priesthood, Prophetic ministry and Kingship, Christ instituted a ministerial priesthood which, in a profoundly true sense, exists because there are laymen and one that (unlike the fundamental priesthood of all the faithful) will end with the completion of its temporal function among the wayfaring faithful.

Through the Pope, bishops and priests, Christ organizes his people, and supplies them with the means—Sacrament, Word and Pastorate—whereby they can do the will of his Father in themselves and in total human history. By his Spirit and the sacramental action of the imposition of hands (1 Tm. 4:14), he has given to the members of the episcopal college, all successors of the Apostles, the plenitude of his priesthood, making them the true pastors of his people (Mt. 18:18; 28:19–20), not merely administrators, but animators (Bishop Emile-Joseph De Smedt). To the Sovereign Pontiff, successor of St. Peter, the Rock (Mt. 16:18), he has entrusted responsibility over the universal Christian community (Mt. 16:18–19; Jn. 21:19; Lk. 22:32). Moreover, he has empowered the members of the episcopal college to ordain priests (Acts 14:22) to collaborate with them in the local realization of their apostolic mission. Those who have received the sacrament of Orders are ordained to imitate Christ as servants of his people (Mt. 10:42–45) and stewards of God's mysteries (1 Cor. 4:1–2). In fulfillment of the divine promise and command (Mal. 1:11; Lk. 22:19), they make present, in liturgical rite, the redeeming

Sacrifice of Christ in the midst of his people, so that all may exercise their priesthood by uniting themselves with the supreme act of the Savior. They distribute the vivifying fruits of Christ's Sacrifice among the faithful through the sacraments, the mysterious, effective signs of salvation. Commissioned to safeguard and teach the deposit of faith (Lk. 10:16), and promised the protection and guidance of the Spirit of Truth (Jn. 14:16) "even to the consummation of the world" (Mt. 28:20), the Magisterium of the ecclesiastical hierarchy advances Christ's people in the knowledge of his revealed Word, to which all are committed to bear witness in their daily lives. And they are enjoined to strengthen the faithful (Lk. 22:32) so that they may endure "the burden of the day's heat" (Mt. 20:12) in the undertaking of the gigantic enterprise that is uniquely theirs, that of sanctifying the profane world of the City of Man in all its dimensions—their special contribution to the extension of the Kingdom of God.

So it happens that in the Economy of Salvation that, while all members of the Church are "the Body of Christ, member for member" (1 Cor. 12:27–28), they have different functions in the Christian community according to the grace that has been given to them individually (Rom. 12:6). And basic to these complementary vocations within the Church is the distinction between cleric and layman (1 Cor. 3:9), one that is adapted to man's nature, and part of the incarnational dynamic of Christ's redeeming mission.

But this, most assuredly, is not a polarization within the Church's organic structure—*sacerdotes* and *idiotes,* as some would have it: the clerical experts and, set over against them in a far-removed realm of being, separated by an impassable gulf, the submerged laity, defined by the secular interpretation of the term as the non-specialists.

The status of the laity in the Church is no vestigal position, one negatively determined by the fact that they have not received the sacrament of Holy Orders. Contrary to the mentality of Constantinian clericalism, Christ never intended the laity to be mere passive, "whispering" objects of a harassed or patronizing ecclesiastical care and direction. He has united them mystically to himself, making them, as we have emphasized, sharers in a limited, analogical, but authentic manner, in his Priesthood, Prophetic ministry, and Kingship; and he has made them co-responsible for the continuation of his threefold mission in the warp and woof of history. Their role is, in fact, irreplaceable in the humanization, sanctification and consecration of the "profane" world, over which the hierarchy has no immediate control, and to which it has no direct access. "Through them," declared Pope Pius XII, "the Church is the vital principle of human society." There are even sectors of the hierarchy's specific apostolate (such as the promotion of Christian education and diocesan-parish organizations) which, in the prevailing conditions of human society, often need the mandated assistance of a trained Catholic laity. Moreover, Karl Rahner, S.J., reminds us, the "so-called layman, by reason of his baptismal membership, can be and often enough really has been, no less than the clergy, the gateway and the antenna" of the Church's charismatic element in action, belief, and love, under the immediate influence of the Spirit, who does not always and necessarily proceed through institutional channels. He would have us further recall that "the laity are and must be to a great extent the carriers" of the necessary public opinion (as Pope Pius XII called it) in the universal Church.

Happily, our century is witnessing the emergence of the articulate, active Christian layman, a fact vigorously manifest, for example, in the recent, extraordinary development of

Catholic Action and the Lay Missionary movement. The Catholic layman's rediscovery of his magnificent vocation is decidedly one of today's singular enrichments to the Church.

But let it be insisted that all this is far removed from laicism, the counterpart of clericalism, both calamitous evils. There is no question here of depreciating the gradation of rank (instituted by Christ and "totally directed to certain, definite ecclesiastical-social functions") in the structure of the Church; nor the fact that "the strictly apostolic ministry in its institutional form keeps its priority . . . and that all the other ministries must be carried on in communion with it, and in the end be judged by it, in the name of the Spirit of Christ" (P. A. Liège, O.P.). Rather, it is the exciting re-discovery of what Christ intends should be the Christian layman's vocation and, for that matter, the occasion for the priest's more profound insight into his own anointed dignity and sacred mission. For, as Louis and André Rétif observed, "the increasingly effective presence of a genuine laity reveals the true nature of the priest's proper function in the Church . . . Through repeated, judicious, and mutual contacts between priest and layman, the former achieves his own unity in a total personal commitment, involving genuine responsibilities and a dynamic forward movement that are involved in his vocation as such."

By vital communion with a genuine laity (one increasingly aware of its Christian commitment and the agonizing needs of our time) those who are chosen and consecrated in the Sacrament of Holy Orders become more fully alert to the clamoring "demand for priests who are fully men and men who have become fully priests; priests who are alive in the full sense of the word, who learn from the school of life and the voice of the Spirit;" priests who will avoid the many subtle obsessive alibis and substitutes for their sacred trust, and truly become "men consumed" in incandescent, loving service to Christ and his brethren.

Significantly, as displayed in dramatic strength throughout the Second Vatican Council, the remarkable contemporary development of the Catholic lay movement coincides with a deepening, appreciative insight into the mystery of the episcopate collegiality—of the Pope's mission as the vital summit of the Church's unity, and of the mission of the bishops who in union with the Sovereign Pontiff (from whom they immediately receive their jurisdiction) and duly subordinate to his authority, are true successors of the apostles and direct representatives of Jesus Christ in their respective dioceses. The profound fact that the Church is built around them is, without doubt, becoming a dynamic, strengthening element in the ecclesial awareness of today's apostles.

Also more clear in the focus of consciousness of the genuine Christian is the singular splendor and incomparable inherent value of the "religious state;" that of those men and women who, by way of the evangelical counsels, of poverty, chastity and obedience, consecrate themselves to God by public vow. Within the many-faceted Mystical Body of Christ, the sublime vocation of religious (and members of "Secular Institutes") is to offer Almighty God the most unconditional form of loving service. Having perceived that "we have no abiding city" (Heb. 13:13–14) and eager to lose their existence to the things of this world for Christ's sake (Mt. 16:24–25), their lives of contemplation and work become signs of possible eschatological triumph, of Christ's grace already victorious in the here-and-now of history.

In sum, all the members of the Church have not the same function, but have different gifts according to the grace that has been given them; yet all, though many, are "one Body in Christ" (Rom. 12:4–8). And all, united with Christ their Head, and participating in his Priesthood, his Prophetic ministry, and his Kingship, are engaged (each one according to his state of life) in the mighty work of the Church's apostolate, providing the Holy Spirit with the human love and thought and emotion and imagination and action, whereby the mystical New Man (Eph. 2:15) advances through history, raising all creation in glory to his Father!

9 * Challenge

When written in Chinese, the word "crisis" is composed of two characters—one represents danger and one represents opportunity.

John F. Kennedy

Every moment is the now of responsibility, of decision.

Rudolf Bultmann

Let Him easter in us, be a dayspring to the dimness of us, be a crimson-cresseted east.

Gerald Manley Hopkins, S.J.

He who hesitates is like a wave of the sea, driven and carried about by the wind.

(James 1:6)

IN RETROSPECT, within the complex currents of change that sweep along contemporary mankind, we recall the two overall drives: man's growing consciousness of the heights and depths of his own individual person, and his awakening to the meaning of his solidarity with the entire human race. Parallel to these advances we remark the increasing awareness of Christians to the significance of their vocation and to the supernatural unity of the Church.

It would seem that mankind as a whole had a presentiment of the profound stirrings of renovating grace within the Mystical Body of Christ. Actually, it is this same divine impulse of the Holy Spirit that has released far-reaching energies within the human totality. Virtue goes out from the Church, attracting, guiding, animating, divinizing. The Finger of God penetrates all history, both sacred and profane. The perception of this truth renders history—otherwise bewilderingly enigmatic—a transparency in whose dark light we come to recognize that, within the present crises of growth, and beneath the evil as well as the good that the Spirit himself inspires, Divine Providence sovereignly directs the massive historical evolution.

We must recognize the momentous truth that the end of total history is the building up of the Mystical Body of Christ; and that it is humanity (and through humanity, all creation), plunged in time-space duration, that century by century provides Christ with the material for his Body—analogous to the manner in which Mary, our youngest sister, provided the flesh and the blood for the physical Christ. This is the successive preparation that continues in our era, in our day. Now, within the heightening perspectives of the twofold awareness within the Church and within humanity, as both Christ's Body and mankind open on to new dimensions and maturity, the Church progressively transforms the world by purifying and absorbing all that is good in the emerging forces, sloughing off all that is sin, rehabilitating all in Christ.

But the imminent danger is that the sublime work of the Church be impeded by our sloth and interference, and that the two powerful drives within contemporary mankind be used by the powers of evil instead of being assimilated and developed by the Holy Spirit through our very being an apostolate. Confronted by the exigencies of the new historical developments, we remain in satisfied slumber and dreamy dignity while the encroachment of the agents of Satan into the shaping of mankind and the evolving cosmos takes on fantastic proportions.

There are the millions who, plumbing the deep and wide reaches of their personal being, but without the light of Christ, are overcome by the vertigo of their own inscrutability, and by "an excessive sense of evil that breeds a guilt . . . the kind that leads to submission to anything." Instead of discovering the burgeoning of their personality in Christ, who knows their personal mystery (Jn. 2:25), and calls them by name (Is. 43:1), they seek themselves among the dead (Lk. 24:5).

They follow ersatz "mysticisms" that promise life's fulfillment, only to discover that visions, no matter how dynamically splendid, are not enough. Their very nature demands a living focus, a vital embodiment of the orientations that rise within their being: they need a Person. And so they seek to find the meaning of their deepest ego in someone who summarizes in himself, with consummate, translucent power, all the mysteries of man's nature and destiny. But instead of being introduced to the God-Man, Christ Jesus, they desperately submit themselves to the blind guidance of false prophets.

And there are the millions who, without the articulated guidance of Christ, are propelled by the mysterious drive towards human solidarity in a tormenting passion, an upsurge of ideals that, straining beyond barriers, often gropes wildly in tragic violence. They give themselves in total commitment,

not to the building up of the living and vivifying Body of
Christ, the realization of mankind's unity, but to the erection
of totalitarian bodies that are from their inception things of
disintegration, disillusionment. Because we do not cooperate
with the Holy Spirit in the channeling of these radically valid
aspirations within the countless persons that constitute the
masses, their energies continue to be consumed parasitically by
international movements that ape, with diabolical perversion
and blasphemy, the very characteristics of Christ's Mystical
Body.

For very many of us are indifferent to the implications of
the truth expressed by Henri de Lubac: that "it is through
Christ that the person reaches maturity . . . that man
emerges definitely from the universe, and becomes conscious
of his own being." We pass over this revelation that we are
fully persons only when, as living members of Christ's Body
—sharing vitally in the rhythm of being and action, of contemplative and sacramental life, of liturgy and apostolate, and
in its honest insertion into the palpable "spunslime" of
present history—we commune with the transfigured humanity
of Jesus Christ, and thereby share in the very life of the
Blessed Trinity. Instead of being "other Christs" to our brethren, we present them instead with eviscerated Christian lives,
that repel, and even evoke pity, rather than attract.

Again, in practice very many of us treat as esoteric the doctrine of the Mystical Body of Christ. We still view our encounter with God within cramping individualistic perspectives, believing, with Peter Nicole (died 1695), that "a man is
created to live alone with God forever." The fact of our
solidarity with all redeemed mankind in Christ's Church fails
to shake us from our selfish somnolence.

This amounts to the staggering failure on our part to recognize Christ himself—the Lord whose human features bear the stamp of our "Today."

Moreover, because of our aloof uprootedness from the cosmos of people and things in which we move and because of our lack of concern for its numerous values, very many of us do not really recognize our contemporary world-citizens. We disregard the fact that not only is man called to make history; the orientation of his personality is deeply conditioned by history. He acts in history, history acts on him. This being so, the phenomenon that must not be overlooked (though it may hardly be apparent by reason of our actual involvement in its flux) is the unfathomable influence exerted by the new rhythms and aspirations on human persons in the immediate historical context—a context that is the outcome of vast modifications through past centuries, but that is unique in itself. Consequently, to recognize our contemporary brethren—who are, in a very special way our brethren, our charge—we must strive to know the contours of the historical mold in which their personalities (and ours, despite our unawareness) are being shaped considerably. We must perceive and appreciate its multiform values through the revealing power of humility and charity.

But because so many of us are negligent in this paramount duty, our neighbors are strangers to us, and we to them. There is no empathy, no rapport. And this lamentable estrangement obtains even between us and our brethren of the same milieux.

In sum, we neither truly know Jesus Christ nor our fellow humans. We form a deadweight humanity that impedes the providential advance of history. We hinder and slow down the full actualization of the "Second Pentecost," and thereby the growth of Christ's Mystical Body and the return of our divine Lord.

One is here reminded of Paul Claudel's poetic interpretation of the first Pentecost. "From end to end the Holy Scriptures can find no better way of representing the direct effect of God on the soul than by the operation of fire, . . . Ezechiel even goes so far as to compare it to an electrical phenomenon. . . . It is used to represent that God who appeared to Moses in the burning bush. 'For the Lord, your God, is a consuming fire,' we are told in Deuteronomy (4:24), and again in the Epistle to the Hebrews, in Exodus, and in the theophanic prophecies. 'The glory of the Lord was seen as a consuming fire' (Ex. 24:17). Fire is the element that seizes, surrounds and penetrates; it is the outward form and inward quality of love. Its attributes are heat, light, penetration, merciless examination, and destruction. It is the medium through which God appears and communicates with us, by which he expresses himself, searches us, sounds us, smells us, tastes us, holds us fast, speaks to us, questions us, expands us, and embraces us. . . . This is the fire which inflamed the twelve Apostles on the day of Pentecost, and transformed them into inextinguishable torches; the flame that suddenly broke forth over their heads on that holy day *was the emanation of their own souls which, having arrived at a supreme state of vibration, burst into being at the touch of the divine spark.*"

Claudel, fully cognizant of the initiative of the Holy Spirit, was anxious to bring into focus the wonder of human cooperation with the fiery burst of the divine action, and also he wished to stress the creativity of this divinizing fire within the apostles: for the Virgin Mary, Spouse of the Holy Spirit, "fashioned all these varied hues into a single bolt, sending them back to heaven in a flaming spiral." The sacred lightning transformed fruitfully the men gathered with Mary, their

Queen, and, then, accompanied as it were by the thunderclap of accomplishment, returned to heaven and the bosom of God.

The same primordial fire of the Spirit descends upon us in our moment of history. But it will consume and transfigure and create in full measure, only through wholehearted co-operation with the Divine Spirit. For God respects our freedom—even when we fail to use it profitably.

10 * Values

A new age of Christendom if it is to come, will be an age of reconciliation of that which was disjoined, the age of a "secular" Christian civilization, in which temporal things, philosophical and scientific reason, and civil society will enjoy their autonomy and at the same time recognize the quickening and inspiring role that spiritual things, religious faith, and the Church play from their higher plane. Then a Christian philosophy of life would guide a community vitally, not decoratively Christian, a community of human rights and of the dignity of the human person, in which men belonging to diverse racial stocks and to diverse spiritual lineages would work at a temporal common task which was truly human and progressive.

Jacques Maritain

In the old days, on Easter night, the Russian peasants used to carry the blest fire home from church. The light would scatter and travel in all directions through the darkness and the desolation of the night would be pierced and dispelled as lamps came on in

*the windows of the farm houses, one by one. Even
so the glory of God sleeps everywhere, ready to blaze
out unexpcetedly in created things. Even so His
peace and His order lie hidden in the world, even
the world of today, ready to re-establish themselves
in His way, in His own good time: but never without the instrumentality of free options made by free
men.*

Thomas Merton

In his Christmas message of 1956, Pius XII summoned
Christians to confront today's new-world-in-the-making, and to
"take their stand on the firm ground of nature and faith, courageously yet prudently re-assessing the values involved, primarily those which are in man himself."

This is our duty and privilege. We are to enlarge our personalities in Christ (become truly *Catholic*), deepen our
confidence in Divine Providence, and root ourselves in the
present historical complex. We must help open the prism of
contemporary creation—all the facets of mankind and the cosmos that are being specially focused in our day—and place
them beneath the "rays of life and immortality" that Christ
sheds abroad (2 Tm. 1:10). In other words, we must search
out and rediscover the innumerable spiritual riches within the
contemporary historical ferment, and integrate them into the
total coherence of the Church's vision and mission. For these
values, though open to idolatrous misuse as absolutes, are in
themselves genuine and noble. They open to God, and find
their fulfillment only in God. Within today's convulsed rage
for life and personal identity, there burns a profound longing
for the One who is himself Life (Jn. 14:6); and within the
worldwide, groping movements toward socialization and unity
there is present an uprush of human spirit toward the ideal of
supernatural brotherhood in Christ. Contemporary human

values are providential elements in God's twofold Design of Creation and Redemption, "points of insertion" through which, with our cooperation, the purifying, divinizing energies of the Holy Spirit enter into the bloodstream of human existence.

We have already indicated the profound movements toward personal and communal fulfillment within contemporary mankind—two advances, we suggested, that coincide as persentiments with analogous, supernatural advances within the Church.

It remains for us to look deeper into the currents of transformation that now criss-cross our globe, and to detect in their ambiguity some of the values that await the Christian leaven. We have chosen to study briefly three of the most important. We can only indicate the bold, careful work that must be undertaken by Christians in the harvest of these weed-ridden, human values: but even a summary will reveal its urgency and earnestness and splendor.

Overall, it appears that in the nightmarish accelerated world of pain and rapture and chaos and creativity in which he now exists, man's being is bared to the quick and burnished, "worn down even to the soul." In this state of heightened suggestibility, he is malleable to the forces of good and evil as seldom before in history. His mind and sensibilities may be kneaded into pre-arranged patterns by systematized, perverted propaganda (the subtle regimentation of word stimuli, whose power Pavlov already recognized), and by the conditioning strategy whose effectiveness has been proven, in shocking, concentrated form, by recent tyrannical "brainwashing" programs.

We need only recall the consummately degrading transformation of the anti-Nazi mayor of Weimar into the chained, barking watchdog at the Büchenwald gate.

This is the rape of man's very soul that reaches terrifying proportions in the mass paronoia of Totalitaria, the horror depicted in the dark pages of Franz Kafka's novels.

On the other hand, to an unprecedented degree contemporary man is open to education in human maturity. Even the therapy that may be employed to destroy the image of God in his being can also be used to help him overcome many of his limitations and develop the many facets of his personality. His present susceptibility can be opened, in mature freedom, to the stimulus of Divine grace. Our age is, in fact, an age of exciting opportunity for the education of mankind in its fully human, supernatural Christian vocation.

There is contemporary man's deepening consciousness of the "burden and glory of freedom" (J. F. Kennedy).

This fact finds poignantly eloquent expression in the great crusade for human emancipation that now sweeps our globe. It is true that the new upsurge of passion for liberty often bursts into blind, anarchical fury; and that often its idealism, groping desperately, is betrayed and misdirected by irresponsible mob leaders into regimes of monstrous dehumanization. But essentially it is a noble, a holy cause, one whose inherent aspiration is directed toward the opening up of the dignified freedom of all persons, irrespective of their many differences. The individual who is not moved by such yearnings of his brothers and sisters for the rich integrity of their personal being certainly does not deserve the name Christian—nor human.

The growing consciousness of freedom has another aspect to its progress. Not only must man be delivered from human injustice, but also from cumbrous legacies of the past. He is surrounded and compelled by newness. Everything has become provisional.

We have already alluded to the crucial danger of his slipping from fundamental traditional moorings, and becoming lost in a vortex of change—doomed, as Lord Acton warned, to repeat mistakes. But beyond the corrosion of continuity with the past and the fevered turmoil in newness and the bizarre, there is discernible man's dawning appreciation that not a little of tradition—its categories of thought and its pragmatic lessons—is irrelevant to the immediate world of unprecedented innovation; and that he must, in full freedom, contemplate the uniqueness of Today afresh, and assimilate and shape its newness to human ends. More and more he realizes that it may very well be that "radical actions will be the most genuinely conservative, by preserving key values in drastically changed circumstances" (Henry Wriston).

The issue that we wish to emphasize is the fact that contemporary man is advancing in deep awareness that God has, to an unprecedented degree, "left him in the hand of his own counsel" (Eccl. 15:14). Mankind is truly coming of age. This is no guarantee of man's free response to the divine Will; but it is an unfolding of the possibility of his conversion to God and this, in itself, is an unspeakable blessing. Only in the bracing climate of freedom can man "wrestle" with God.

Of course, there are those who, intoxicated by the idea of contemporary mankind's adulthood, foolishly agree with Dietrich Bohhoeffer's claim that "God is teaching us that we must live as men who can get along very well without him." Certainly God wants man to expand in his full humanity, and to outgrow immature modes of thinking and acting. But for one to assert his absolute independence of God, condemning the stalwart admission of fundamental, absolute basic reliance on Divine Providence as unworthy of him, is in itself an indication of abysmal puerility. The fact is that man, in bringing to fruition his tremendous capabilities, perfects the image of

God within him, and reveals with increasing depth his essential, constant dependence on his Creator.

Is it not significant that within the Church itself this century is witnessing an emancipation from the hindrance and insularity of irrelevant categories of thinking and behavior, and a deepening realization of the true liberty of the Christian (Gal. 4:31)? Rahner refers to our era as the "hour of pneumatic individuality." Today's Christian, a member of the Church of the Diaspora, cannot allow his belief and practice to become mere products of tradition and environment; things to believe and do because of upbringing and custom. For the most part, the milieu is not Christian: institutions that once might have buttressed his vapid Christian life are absent. To be a Christian is now under God, probably as never before in history, a constant challenge "that we keep our liberty awake, ready at any moment to transcend the stultifying artificiality of common existence with decisions that affirm our inner, spiritual identity as sons of God" (Thomas Merton).

There is also contemporary man's growing sense of *history*, of an evolution in which he himself is involved, not just passively, but actively as a maker. This maturing is evident among the "people" as well as among intellectuals, though its actuality and significance is not sufficiently appreciated.

To quote Gerhard Krüger: "Today history is our biggest problem."

Through painstaking research and discovery contemporary man has pushed back the frontiers of the past and has entered, in a very real sense, into the immediate presence of his earliest ancestors and of remote, ancient civilizations. He has studied with interest the rich, turbulent flow of history, and has attempted, in an amazing number of interpretations, to establish the existence of rhythms and laws within history's movement. At the same time, aided by the new means of communication, he is able to be "on the spot" in the actual history-in-the-making of our day.

As never before he is aware that the pattern of his life is conditioned, to a remarkable degree, by the historical happenings of the moment. He is confident that he can guide these events, and that, from within their germination, he has a vital role to play in the shaping of his own destiny and those of his world neighbors.

This awakening amounts to a profound broadening of man's horizons of vision and aspiration. It means that his soul is increasingly oriented, not only to the drama of humanity in the kaleidoscopic, global history of the concrete present in which he lives, but to the full, momentous sweep of mankind's march to its destiny.

This sense of history is poles apart from the conception of humanity's existence as an eternal, ineluctable renewal; of subjection to a *fatum*, a cycle of causes, influences and effects that are perpetually renewed in every detail. Contemporary man envisages history as having direction—even when he considers its goal an agonizing absurdity.

Communism avails itself of this spiritual experience within contemporary mankind and offers a dialectical philosophy of history, with an assurance of history's triumphant, concrete consummation in time. It provides the individual with a missionary mystique; for each man, by consecrated service to the Communist cause, can contribute to the actualization of the proletarian millennium.

Not a little of Communism's advance is attributable to these historical perspectives that it brings to contemporary man—and to our own inexcusable ennui with the vision of history that the Church would have us make our own and share.

For Christianity is the only religion that recognizes in amplitude the profound significance of history as the successive, linear unfolding of the Divine plan for mankind within time-space duration, and its ultimate emergence in eternity. Its eschatological theology of history is no mere structure of abstract ideas, but a truly existential grappling with reality; for Christianity is, in essence, an *Event*. It experiences the life-process of history as a dynamic thrust forward toward the recapitulation and transformation of all mankind and creation in the Lord—an impelling progress of astounding grandeur, replete with happenings that relate to each other across the ages; a tremendous movement in which all of us are called to participate under the energizing guidance of the Holy Spirit.

Whereas Communism shrinks man's role in history and his terminal destiny to confines of time and space, Christianity opens both to the infinite reaches of eternity. True, man lives in time-space; this is his misery and his greatness, his duty and his privilege. But through time-space he can penetrate the very heavens: he can be a missionary of both the finite and the infinite!

It is significant that the Church today is experiencing an amazing revival of interest in the Bible, a "rediscovery" of sacred history that is intimately a part of the deepening sense of history throughout contemporary mankind. Both histories, sacred and secular are intertwined in the concrete reality of mankind's existence: confronting one of them is, in fact, an approach to the other also; and both invite man to engagement in the mystery of divine Providence.

In sum, the new historical awareness is, unquestionably, a unique opportunity for mankind to be introduced to the Christian Event that advances through the ages, the Event in which already they, unknowingly, are involved. Contemporary man seeks personal identity and meaning; and it is only within

the context of this sacred history that his search can be fruitful.

There is moreover contemporary man's discovery of his
mounting power not only over the material world, but over his
own human existence; and his realization that more than ever
must he become a being of alert, spiritual responsibility.
"The day before yesterday," Gaston Berger has commented,
"we unconsciously followed what we called Nature. Yesterday
we tried conscientiously to conform to Nature. But today, our
power having grown considerably, it behooves us to protect
Nature, and sometimes to arrange it in ways that seem favorable. We have somehow become responsible for evolution
. . . A reality is to be constructed, rather than events
awaited."

A century ago, man considered himself enveloped and
sheltered by an absolute Nature. Today he is aware of its awe-
someness as never before; but he now *confronts* nature, knowing that he can channel and wield its energies and shape its
forms; and he comprehends that he must even protect it—not
so much from its own ferocity, but from his unscrupulous misuse of its seemingly infinite potentialities.

It may be justifiably claimed that contemporary man has
entered into a "dialogue" with nature, using new symbols for
communication.

Of course, it will be argued that the scientific instruments
and the machines encapsulate man from contacting the realities of the material world. And it is undeniable that the
human person today is all too frequently out of touch with the
tangible extension and qualities of things, their individuality
and their myriad relationships. But may this not be ascribed to
his difficulty in adjusting right away to his new mode of relationship with nature?

"The control over matter allows man to rediscover a concrete sense of the world's creation," Father M. D. Chenu observes. Indeed, it would appear that contemporary man communicates with matter in its innermost vitals, and that he is more cognizant of its splendid, existential mystery.

He is learning to approach the realm of matter with a profound sense of dedication to its study and proper use—a fact proven by, among other things, the extraordinary asceticism and "pursuit of efficiency" with which he applies himself to research and construction.

In other words, he is realizing more and more (even if still vaguely) that his vocation is to be a "co-creator" with God in the fabulous work of Creation.

Contemporary man is also increasingly conscious of his power over human life and destiny—his own and others.

Only recently he has been bitterly awakened to the odious defilement and massacre of humanity that the misuse of power can produce. He is still haunted by the unimaginable horrors of Auschwitz, Dachau, Buchenwald, Ravensbrück. Even now he sees his fellowman debased and slaughtered under bloodstained, power-gorged tyrannies. The possibilities for monstrous cruelty lurking in his being have been unmasked to an unprecedented degree.

But it is incontrovertible that from within mankind there now arises a determined, effective aspiration to employ powerful organization (centralized politically and militarily) in the furtherance of man's total welfare, rather than in his enslavement. Specifically, there is evident in contemporary mankind an advancing, enlightened responsibility that confronts, with balanced realism and unflinching initiative, the enormous issues at stake in the new expansion and intensification of governmental control.

It is a militant alertness to the alarming, unethical encroachment of so many recent governments into personal life. "Governments have taken the place of people. They have also taken the place of God. Government speaks for the people, dreams for them, and determines, absurdly, their lives and deaths . . ." (Ben Hecht).

At the same time, it includes a prudent realization that "even with the most favorable possible outcome, that is, maximum justice, the sphere of the state is going to outweigh that of private life; not because the sphere of private life has shrunk, but because that of the state has expanded, the increased potentialities offered by the present historical situation being such that nothing else but the state could possibly handle them" (Karl Rahner); and that "perhaps the pathological growth of our bureaucracy presents not only a negative symptom of our times, but also a kernel of truth: historical-political conditions are far more malleable now than formerly, and hence must be approached with greater awareness and precision than in the past. All the bumbling bureaucracy may be reflections of the contemporary state's insufficient comprehension of this fact" (Romano Guardini).

Moreover, the new responsibility contains a realistic awareness of the dangers involved in the very attitude of the individual, human person towards the unfolding of governmental power. On the one hand there is "the individual who has become more conscious than ever of his dependence on society. But he does not experience this dependence as a positive asset, an organic tie, but rather as a threat to his natural rights, or even his economic existence. . . . The egotistical drives of his make-up are constantly being accentuated, while his social drives . . . progressively deteriorate" (Albert Einstein). On the other hand, there is the individual who, shirking the burden of human initiative, is glad to live a whole life on credit, satisfied with mere "security," and is only too willing to be controlled by Big Brother.

It is evident that contemporary man's access to power brings with it a commensurate urgency for more growth in individual responsibility. And does not the labyrinth of such responsibility lead ultimately to God?

Again is it not significant that within the Church itself the manifold responsibility for initiative on the part of the individual Catholic is now receiving renewed, extraordinary emphasis?

The fact is that our epoch is experiencing two new maturation processes, one in the Church and one in the world; and both redound to each other, for the Holy Spirit guides both histories. Even the errors in today's world—and there are plenty—contribute accidentally, but existentially, to the growth of Christ's Mystical Body.

It is readily apparent that these human values are interpenetrated by an uncertainty that must be clarified by the Christian. There is a weight within these values-made-flesh that threatens their integral purity, and rushes them to deviation and corruption. They must be courageously purified and redeemed—a purging process that must be accomplished within the soul and flesh of our contemporary world-citizens and institutions, for it is in them that these values are incarnated and develop.

Take for example today's struggle for human freedom. Its purpose is just and noble. This cannot be questioned. If anything, its moral urgency is not sufficiently appreciated by many Christians. But, at the same time, it is indisputable that this engagement very frequently erupts into hatred and bloody violence which, in turn, forge new fetters of enslavement. It is necessary that Christians be the leaven of true liberty within this struggle, literally living centers that radiate the redeeming love of Christ.

This is an exacting, heroic task that can only be fulfilled by the quickening, prudent strength of the Holy Spirit upholding our efforts. But it *can* be done! We have God's word for it (Mk. 10:27).

Do existing conditions warrant optimism for mankind's future?

Romano Guardini has this to say, "All we really know is that where the destructive elements are so violent, historical conditions so precarious, and human attitudes so confused, grounds for pessimism are, to say the least, as solid as for optimism. . . . Nevertheless, I wish to repeat, expressly, that I believe in the possibility of a positive solution—not in the old, liberal sense of letting things 'take care of themselves,' still less in agreement with that historical-dialectical optimism which insists that all things necessarily move toward something better. Such attitudes only endanger the chances of a positive outcome, for they fail to alert these forces on which, ultimately, everything depends: the personal responsibility of free men. I am convinced that such freedom has a real chance to swing history into a happier direction."

Under God, everything depends on the personal responsibility of free men!

And among the free, are not we who are baptized in Christ, by vocation the most free (2 Cor. 3:17)? It is we in particular who are entrusted with the enormous enterprise of sorting out and developing and defending the genuine values of our era, providential "sacraments"—what we may call "sacraments of history"—through which contemporary man moves nearer to Christ, and irreplaceable "material" that we of today must provide for the building up of the Mystical Body of Christ.

It is a holy work. It is one that we can hopefully undertake through cooperation with the Holy Spirit who is, in fact, the ultimate, fecundating, transforming source of all true, historical renewal.

Wellsprings

11 ✳ God the Father

The waters saw Thee, O God,
the waters trembled at the sight of Thee,
moved to their inmost depths;
. . . Thy crackling thunders rolled,
till all the world shone with Thy lightnings,
and the troubled earth shook.
Thy way led through the sea,
the deep tide made a road for Thee,
and none may read the traces of Thy passage.

(Ps. 76:17–20)

For God so loved the world as to give His
only-begotten Son.

(Jn. 3:16)

In this manner, therefore, shall you pray:
'Our Father . . .'

(Mt. 6:9)

THE uniquely perfect generation is in God, for the First Person of the Blessed Trinity is the origin of the Second Divine Person. "From the Father alone is the Son, not made, not created, but begotten" (Athanasian Creed). "From the womb, before the day star I begot thee" (Ps. 109:3).

The Almighty Father is Paternity in his entirety, existing in his very relation as Father to the Son. It is he who, in infinite generosity, gives the Divine Nature to the Second Person, his substantial Image (Col. 1: 15). And the mutual exchange of their intense love is the Third Person, the Gift who, in turn, gives himself in an everlasting movement of love, to both the Father and the Son. The Father is, therefore, the source of the "community of the most perfect individuality," the Blessed Trinity.

Now the eternal, infinite fecundity of the First Person is absolutely spiritual, an intellectual generation of the Word, utterly encompassed by divine love. From this mystery at the center of all causation derives and divides, through successive orders of being, all fertility. Above all, there is the incomparable communication of divine life to mankind through the mysterious marriage of divine and human natures in Christ, and the supernatural fecundity of the mystical nuptuals of the Savior and his immaculate Spouse, the Church. Again, there is the sacrament of Christian marriage, the Mystical Body in miniature, the efficacious symbol that re-presents the vital, organic union of Christ and his Church.

The amazing truth is that we, through authentic apostolate, participate in a real, analogous manner, in the divine fruitfulness. For through the quickening power of the Holy Spirit (who watches over all generation of being, supernatural as well as natural), and motivated by love of God, we share in the rich fecundity of the Church. Like St. Paul, we beget others in Christ (Gal. 4:2). Instead of living an existence of uneventful impotency, we become, in a mysterious derived sense, co-creators with the Father Almighty.

This is our mission that has its origin in the First Person of the Trinity. For it was the Father who, loving man with divine extravagance despite his sin, sent his only begotten Son to redeem us (1 Jn. 4:9–10). And as the Father sent Christ, so Our Lord sends us, his Church (Jn. 20:21) to cooperate with his Spirit in the communication of divine life to all mankind, the life that ultimately comes from the divine Paternity.

The Father is also the fountainhead of holiness—a profound fact that we tend to forget, with lamentable consequences.

Our God is no mere impersonal absolute. Even the Marxian philosophy recognizes an absolute matrix of reality in matter's blind, inexorable evolution. Rather, our God is the numinous Divinity of religion, the living, personal Lord of faith. He is the God who is holy, *sanctum* (Is. 1:4), perfect above all perfection, in whose presence all creation is unclean, and before whose ineffable excellence humble adoration is the inescapable condition. He is the Holiness before whom the hierarchy of angels (Eph. 1:21), numbering thousands upon thousands (Dn. 7:10), adore with heavenly liturgy (Ap. 5:8; 7:11–12). He is the luminous Purity who invaded our numb, grey existence in Christ's Transfiguration and Resurrection. He is the One whom the radiant innocence of little children reflect (Mt. 18:10).

Unfortunately, engulfed as we are in a materialistic environment that grows increasingly lethal to vital religious practice, we have allowed the mystery of God's transcendent holiness to be eclipsed in our intelligence and sensibilities. Living in a society wherein God is more and more "prudently relegated to the department of public oratory," we permit him but a meager existence, and forget the shattering reality of his nature.

Of course, we profess outrage at the militant atheism of this "late hour of history." We are deeply affronted by the anti-gospel of a Nietzsche, and his burial of a demised God in the "sweet-smelling caves" of our churches. We scorn Kafka's ominous, despairing refusal to be guided by the "sinking hand" of Christianity. We are forced to concede that in many Christian churches throughout the world, the "roof is open to the daylight, and the rain of heaven wets the face of the kneeling believers"—but we doggedly claim that our God lives, and that true believers are still very much in evidence.

But the truth is that by succumbing to the poisonous secularism of our time we have come to ignore God as God. We have reversed values, Cardinal Suhard shrewdly observed, "grafting God on man, and not man on God." The "meaning of Man" has taken the place of the "meaning of God." He is of interest only insofar that he relates to us, not as he is in himself. He has become marginal, for the most part irrelevant, dismissed to the "rumpus room" of our lives (and our apostolate), as Father Gustave Weigel aptly put it. And when we do allow him entrance into our "daily chain of gestures," we do so out of pragmatic necessity. Not only must he be marginal, he must be functional. No longer is he the All-Holy Triune God, the "Otherness," as Karl Barth writes, but the Deity-made-in-the-image-of-man who waits a block or two away until we happen to recall his presence, and when we feel we desperately need him.

And while we grow more and more insensitive to the holiness of God and immunized to his consecrating presence, we proportionately forget the sacred character of our apostolate. We come to treat it as a kind of sacrosanct business, of which we ourselves are the executives and public-relations officials, members of an ecclesial "Power Elite." We act as though our reply to the anguished question of Albert Camus: "Can men become saints without God?" would be an indifferent "Yes." Fundamentally, we do not realize enough that God's creation and re-creation of man are both hallowed works, of which we are totally unworthy apart from his divine grace.

Likewise we allow the awareness of the sacredness of the individual person to become stifled in our soul. Certainly, we are repelled by the grotesque definition of a human being in one

of Sartre's novels: "A gelatinous job done in a dark room
. . . a bit of thinking flesh that screams and bleeds when it is
killed." But it is indisputable that many of us, who claim to be
Christ's apostles, ignore the unique, unexchangeable dignity of
the persons among whom we are sent, and approach them, not
in humility, but as petty, arrogant Grand Inquisitors who con-
descend to move among the "much-too-many," the "superfluous masses," expecting of them sheep-like submissiveness.

We who allow our sense of God's holy presence to become
increasingly atrophied, forget that man bears such a plenitude
and concentration of being that, in relation to his Creator, he
is the "image and glory of God" (1 Cor. 2:7), even the most
degenerate who subsists beneath the tangled sleaziness of evil;
for deep within his being the Spirit awaits, and seeks to insti-
gate, the slightest movement towards conversion from sin. In
principle he is redeemed in the sacrificial splendor of our Lord.
His transcendent destiny is to be filled with all the fullness of
God (Eph. 3:19), faithfully reflecting the essence of God's
being (Mt. 5:48). He is the creature of love whose ultimate
law of existing is the return of love. The Almighty God values
him, and calls him by name.

But by omission if not by commission, and under the self-
deceptive façade of righteousness, presuming to have God
himself as our accomplice, we profane the divine image in persons. We actually contribute to the contemporary monstrous
drive towards the annihilation of all that is genuine in man,
individual and collective—the diabolical movement that
assaults man surreptitiously or by frontal, violent attack, and
divests him of his sacred dignity. Satan, the Murderer from
the beginning (Jn. 8:44), wildly essays to profane God's holiness by destroying his image in man—and we, unprofitable
servants, help him! In our paltriness we become "God-killers."

It is absolutely essential that we grow in the awareness of God's holiness by prayerful recollection of his presence. Without supernatural reverence—nobly mirrored on the natural plane in the monumental piety of the ancient Greeks—our interior life and the apostolate become a mockery of God's will. This is why Christ commanded us to be perfect like our heavenly Father (Mt. 5:48), and why, on the night before he died, he prayed that we remain holy (Jn. 17:9–26). This is why St. Paul eagerly reminds us that our very bodies are temples of God's Spirit (1 Cor. 6:19–20).

"Loose, saith he, the shoes from off thy feet; for the place whereon thou standest is holy" (Jos. 5:16). We must bear in mind that God wishes us to shed the many pretenses that insult our very being so that the light and power of his holiness cannot filter through to us. "Nor can foot feel, being shod!" As the barefoot man who is intimately in contact with the place on which he walks—the feel of grass, warmth and of shadows—appreciates many sensations denied to the one who is shod, so we, too, when directly open to his nearness, in his members and in his work, will discover new, rich dimensions to our lives that are, till then, neutral, unremittingly moribund.

It would be well for us to set before ourselves the example of the angelic hosts. As we have noted above, they are the *Liturgi* who, in utter self-effacement, adore the Holy Triune God. But they are also the *Angeli*, the messengers who minister between the divinity and our creation. During the long night before the Incarnation, they prepared for the coming of the Emmanuel (Gen. 18, ff; Gal. 3:1; Gal. 3:19). They were present at every crucial moment of Christ's life on earth. And as Origen so ably discussed, they continue to prepare (cooperating with the Holy Spirit and his spouse, Mary) for the coming of Christ into every person, every nation, every age. They are our personal guardians; they protect our attempts in the apostolate. But withal, they behold the face of the Father in heaven (Mt. 18:10); they never cease to continue to contemplate the Beatific Vision. "In this," writes Daniélou, "they set before the apostle the ideal he must always be tending towards, of perfect union and contemplation. . . . action totally bound up in God's will."

12 * The Word made Flesh

I am the Way, the Truth, and the Life.

(Jn. 14:6)

Christ Jesus, who has become for us God-given wisdom and justice, and sanctification, and redemption. . . ."

(1 Cor. 1:30)

. . . And yet I am alive! or rather, not I; it is Christ Who lives in me.

(Gal. 3:20)

Who, then, shall separate us from the love of Christ?

(Rom. 8:35)

To be apostles we must be intimately identified with the living Christ. Apart from union with Christ our attempts are utterly devoid of supernatural efficacy (John 15:6). This truth cannot be gainsaid.

It is by entrance into the Church in baptism that we first encounter the Son of God. For the Church is the fullness of Christ, continuing his Paschal Mystery through time and space, ever growing towards his perfect stature (Eph. 4:14). He is the Head of this Mystical Body, through which he reconciles in himself to God all creation, visible and invisible (Col. 2:8–10). This is the ineffable secret to which St. Paul constantly returned in eloquent simplicity, the secret that was hidden in the bosom of the Trinity and is now revealed in Our Lord through his Church (Rom. 16:25).

Our confrontation with Christ is not a matter of externals only. It is a mystical engrafting onto Christ, one whereby we become, as Father Odo Casel expressed it, sacramentally "christed." By our immediate, concrete-spiritual contact with the humanity of Our Lord (miraculously not consumed by the divinity with which it is substantially united, as prefigured by the burning bush of the Mosaic vision), divine life rushes into the very essence of our being. We breathe his Spirit into the remotest fibres of our creaturehood. We become "configured" to Our Lord, entering into the very likeness of his contemplation and mission, his Passion and Resurrection (Rom. 6:5), so that Origen (7th Homily on St. Luke) declared with the daring of faith that all the mysteries of Christ continue to be fulfilled in us today.

Not in the light of simple vision but in the dark luminosity of faith is it possible for us to become aware of the tremendous import of these truths. For Christ resurrected continues to manifest his creative presence through signs—just as he did during the interim between his Resurrection and Ascension, coming among his loved ones, yet remaining strangely unrecognizable (Lk. 24:16; and Jn. 20:24–29), revealing himself through signs that were decipherable only in the transparency of faith.

We thus become "alive to God in Christ Jesus" (Rom. 6:11), and "experience Christ," as the Apostolic Constitutions put it, in the sacred signs of the Church's Sacramental cosmos.

So begins and develops, especially through the Sacrament of Christ's Sacrifice, the unique friendship (Jn. 15:15), without which apostolate is not even thinkable, an intimacy of being and action that has its rhythm of discovery, nourishment, growth, fluctuations, crises, strengthening, transformation. Through this friendship not only do we deepen our recognition of the Son of God and our identification with him, we actually find our own selves; we now truly live and function, and we expand to the realities of the human collectivity and the new, transfigured humanity already emerging in Christ's Mystical Body.

This friendship is, consequently, a union of lives, deep and vibrant. In and through the Church (Eph. 4:7–14) we progressively share in Christ's holiness. We are members of the Church that God wishes to be without blemish (Eph. 1:4), the Mystical Body, divine-human organism, that is consistently purified in attack, treachery, humiliation, persecution. Summoned to be holy like our Head (Eph. 1:14), we share in this total purification. And meantime, as our union with Christ, the wellspring of all supernatural activity, becomes more and more interiorized, our apostolic efforts become more intense; for apostolic action is the expression and fulfillment, the incarnation, of our hidden life in Christ.

But there is another aspect of this unique friendship that is of paramount significance for our apostolate, one that is far too frequently ignored: its *actuality*. The Friend whom we encounter and with whom we commune is living (Heb. 12:18–23) in glory at the right hand of the Father (Heb. 8:1), but also in his Mystical Body in this moment of time, in this division of space. Christ is truly our contemporary. Our friendship is no dubious, abstract thing; it is dynamic, it is *now*, rooted organically in the concreteness of the present, while simultaneously piercing eternity.

We know that the rhythm of friendship consists in mutual exchange. In this extraordinary communion Christ, through his Church, gives himself, his glorified humanity and his divinity, and even here in this world that passes, the beginnings of eternal joy in the Trinity. In return we give our own selves through the Church, and in our very being and action, the gamut of temporal existence in which we are plunged: the human solidarity of which we are a living part, in this definite hour of history, in the fabric of this environment.

In effect, the divinely poignant exchange between the Son of God and mankind continues through each one of us. Its continuation in *this* time and in *this* place depends on our cooperation!—on our being united with his Church of today, aware how its eternal dispositions are conditioned by humanity's present exigencies, and reacting with the Church, in its contemplation and apostolate, to these needs; and on our being united with all that is redeemable in the world of today: its dreams, its accomplishment, all except its sin.

This is the dazzling truth perceived by St. Paul (Eph. 4:7–12) when he emphasized that all the graces we are apportioned by the Holy Spirit are given us "for the building up of the Body of Christ"—that is, not merely for the deepening of our own union with Christ, but for the full expansion of the tremendous friendship between God and mankind in which our personal relationships with Christ are contained and upheld.

Within the dimensions of this friendship our apostolate takes on a new richness, a new urgency.

13 * The Holy Spirit

A message to these bones from the Lord: I mean to send my spirit into you and restore you to life. Sinews shall be given you, flesh shall grow on you, and skin cover you; and I will give you breath to bring you life again; will you then doubt the Lord's power? . . . Come, breath of life, from the four winds, and breathe on these slain men to make them live. So I prophesied as he had bidden me and the breath of life came into them, so that they lived again; and all rose to their feet, host upon host of them.

(Ez. 37:5–10)

If anyone does not have the Spirit of Christ, he does not belong to Christ.

(Rom. 8:9)

The spirit through which God created the world by breathing on it (like the priest who with his lips and his lungs forms the letter psi on the baptismal font) continues to move among us. It is the great south wind which has swelled the sails of the Church since the day of Pentecost. Now it is a gale which uproots oak trees, now the enameler's blowpipe, or the sudden incarnation of the irresistible scene of roses. . . . A word, less than that, the shape of a word: it was enough.

Paul Claudel

Iₙ ᴛʜᴇ New Testament we read that Christ sends his Spirit (Jn. 14:16–26), and also sends his Apostles (John 13:16–20; 17:18). Through the mediation of the Holy Ghost and the apostolate of the Church he continues the divine mission entrusted to him by his heavenly Father (John 20:21).

Thus, between these two sendings there is an organic unity, for the Church's apostolate is initiated, sustained, developed and directed by the quickening, interior energy of the *Dynamis*, the Power of God.

This is why the Acts of the Apostles have been called significantly the "Gospel of the Holy Ghost," for the history of the Church is essentially the history of the Holy Ghost at work in the deeps of humanity, the unfolding of the distinct, unique Mission of the Paraclete. From the account of the first manifestation of the Christian apostolate at Pentecost the entire narration of the years of the Church's history is replete with references to the Third Person of the Blessed Trinity. It was in and through the Spirit of Christ that all the Apostles acted (Acts 5:9). It was he who appointed and consecrated them witnesses of Christ (13:2; 16:6–7). He inspired their preaching and deliberations (1 Cor. 2:4–5; Acts 15:28). He protected and guided them (Acts 10:19–20; 16:6–7). He gladdened them throughout all their efforts (13:52). He emboldened them and fortified them (8:29), even to the heroic embracing of martyrdom (7:55). He was the actuating reality, the *Energeia*, who gave supernatural dynamism to their activity. He is the "Lord of the Apostolate."

These facts are of considerable import, for they indicate the mentality and devotion that should be ours, who presently collaborate in the mission of the Church.

First, we must remember that in the unique, subsistent communion of the Triune God, the encounter of the Love of the Father and the Son is so intimate and perfect that it expresses itself in the living, Third Person. The Holy Ghost is the Spirit of both the Father and the Son, the reciprocal exchange of their charity, in whom the movement of Divine Love is eternally quickened.

The Paraclete is thereby the Spirit of Christ (1 Pt. 1:11; Rom. 8:9), the Spirit of Jesus (Acts 16:17; Phil. 1:19; Rom. 8:9–11), the Spirit of the Lord (Acts 5:9; 8:39; 2 Cor. 3:17–18), the Spirit of his Son (Gal. 4:6).

It was the Holy Spirit who stimulated the entire life of Christ, from the very moment of his conception in the womb of Mary until his elevation above the heavens. It was he who introduced Christ to his public, prophetic ministry—in his baptism (Lk. 3:21–23), and to his priestly sacrifice on Calvary—in his Transfiguration (Mt. 17:1–8).

He is the Gift promised by Our Savior (Jn. 16:7), bringing to us all that he has received on our behalf from Christ (16:15). He is the "river of the water of life, coming forth from the throne of God and of the Lamb" (Ap. 22:1)—the abundant new life that Christ had come to give us (Jn. 10:10).

He is, therefore, our Sanctifier who, dwelling in us (1 Cor. 2:12), vivifies all that we do (1 Cor. 2:13), increasingly transforming us in the image of the glorified Christ. The whole Christian life is actually a "life in the Spirit." Its interior development is precipitated by the mysterious motions of the Holy Ghost called Gifts: Wisdom, Understanding, Counsel, Fortitude, Knowledge, Fear and Piety (Is. 11:2–3); and this interior heightening of the divine action manifests itself in external repercussions, in "social outbursts" without which apostolate is impossible: Benevolence, Amiability, Cordiality, Moderation, Sweetness, Longanimity, Patience, Fidelity, Harmony, Restraint, Ingenuousness, and Joy (Rom. 1:17; Gal. 5:22; Eph. 4:2–5; Col. 3:12–15).

A meditative consideration of all these workings of the Holy Spirit in the authentic Christian life, and a corresponding honest appraisal of much of our so-called apostolate, will reveal the lamentable sham of attempts that are not placed under the vitalizing guidance of the Holy Ghost. Instead of balanced, supernaturally fruitful activities, all too often we witness the feverish emergence of "Projects" that, like cancerous growths, feed upon, and thereby diminish, the spiritual health of our Christian communities.

To appreciate more fully the paramount role of the Holy Spirit in the Church's apostolate, in which ours is a participation, we must also view the apostolate as a continuation of Christ's *prophetic ministry*. Already in Old Testament times this ministry of Our Lord was prefigured by the great prophets who witnessed to the eternal truths of the wonderful designs of God by words and works that were not of mere human artifice, but of the Holy Spirit, and by the sufferings that they bore with patient heroism. In the person of Jesus, the prophets of the Old Covenant, represented by John the Baptist, were superseded (John 3:30), and the prophetic outpourings of the Holy Spirit were concentrated in their entirety (Lk. 4: 16–21; 24:18–19). He is the Word and the supreme Miracle who proclaimed in himself (Lk. 8:54), in the power of his speech and the attestation of his works, and in a special manner in the martyrdom of his Passion, the hidden mysteries of God.

This prophetic ministry the Spirit of Christ continues through the members (particularly the hierarchy) of the Catholic Church (Joel 2:28, 32), infusing their words and actions with the supernatural efficacy to move men's hearts. At times he accompanies their speech with unpredictable, extraordinary inspirations and works, even miracles; and confers on them the strength to give testimony to God, above all by martyrdom.

For while the Holy Spirit dwells within the institutional

Church, he remains above its established ministry and sacraments, sovereignly autonomous. The Spirit acts as he wills (1 Cor. 12:11). But always the charismata that he grants are directed to the building up of the Mystical Body, the Church of law and of love (*Mystici Corporis*), and are subject to the objective rule of faith (12:13) and to apostolic authority (14:37–38), the two criteria of unity, as evidenced in St. Paul, the "Apostle by stealth" (Congar). For the Paraclete is the Spirit of Jesus, and effects no other work than that of Jesus.

It is of capital importance that we realize that these effusions of the Holy Spirit—the "surprises of grace" mentioned by Charles Péguy—are still realities. That they may not seem to be so much in evidence in our immediate experience does not indicate the Holy Spirit's withdrawal, but rather our anemic faith in divine Providence and our tardiness in cooperating with the inspiration of the Paraclete. In our absurd self-sufficiency we become unaware of the Divine, pneumatic visitations in our very midst—like Balaam who failed to see the angel of the Lord who was quite evident to the humble donkey (Nm. 22). For the wonderful, thrilling fact remains that our Christian life and apostolate are full of such holy "conjunctures," wherein the Holy Spirit, instead of simply vivifying the messianic system and sacrament instituted by Christ, intervenes unexpectedly as a distinct Person of the Triune God into the melee of our daily lives.

In our Apostolic activities we must again and again enter into the silence of God and seek the counsel and power of the Divine Spirit—mindful of the mysterious silence on earth and in heaven in the interval between the Ascension and Pentecost that preceded the first manifestation of the Church's Mission. For the history we live in—the history that acts upon us and which we help create—is actually the development of the Spirit's re-creation of mankind, and our engagement in this work. It is the continuation of the First Pentecost throughout the ages until the Return of Our Lord.

Only by living in and by and with the Holy Spirit will we be able to set fire to the cosmos by unquenchable zeal, and transform it in the Redemptive Love of the Blessed Trinity. This is how we can effect, in our immediate apocalyptic history, an unprecedented bestowal of grace, a "Second Pentecost."

Otherwise our influence will be that of a spiritual dry-rot, an arid, blasphemous claim to Christian apostolate.

14 ✳ Christ's Mother

Hail, full of grace, the Lord is with thee! . . . Blessed art thou among women, and blessed is the Fruit of thy womb.

(Luke 1:28, 42–43)

Jesus obeyed his Mother. You have read how all that the Evangelists tell us of Christ's hidden life at Nazareth with Mary and Joseph is that "He was subject to them," and "advanced in wisdom and age" (Luke 2: 51–52). Is there anything incompatible with his divinity in this? Certainly not. The Word is made Flesh; he has stooped so far as to take a nature like to ours, sin excepted; he came, said he, "not to be ministered unto, but to minister" (Mt. 20:28); to be "obedient unto death" (Phil. 2:8); that is why he willed to obey his Mother. At Nazareth he obeyed Mary and Joseph, the two privileged beings whom God had placed near him. In a certain measure, Mary shares in the authority of the Eternal Father over his Son's humanity. Jesus could say of his Mother what he said of his Father in Heaven: "I do always the things that please her" (John 8:29).

Abbot Marmion, O.S.B.

THEOLOGIANS often refer interchangeably to our time as the Century of the Church, and again that of Mary. They observe that, while the significance of the Divine Maternity in fifth century Ephesus * provided deeper insight into the mystery of Our Lord's personal being, centering in its relationship to the *physical* Christ, its special import today lies in its relationship to the *Mystical* Christ, furnishing new awareness of his work in space-time duration. This is the fascinating pursuit of soteriology.

They point to the contemporary resurgence in ecclesiological and Marian studies, and to their living embodiment in present-day apostolate. "It is not only that Mariology can profit from Ecclesiology," insists Karl Rahner, S.J.; "Mariology fertilizes Ecclesiology . . . There is a path from Mariology to Ecclesiology; and Christology considered in its concrete content, as it actually is in saving history, *is* Mariology as well, simply because the Word of God in the flesh is from the Virgin; and this very taking of flesh is, immediately and really, saving history." The three great currents within the Church today—the Liturgical, the Marian and that of the Apostolate —are, in fact, three aspects of the one vital mystery, the profound reciprocity and interlacing of graces between the Mystical Body of Christ and the Mother of Christ.

For "the links between Our Lady and the Church are not only numerous," writes Henri de Lubac, "they are essential

* . . . where, in 421 Mary was infallibly proclaimed Theotokos, Mother of God, the name that "contains the whole mystery of the Incarnation" (John Damascene, *de Fide Orthodoxa*).

and woven from within: they are one single and unique mystery." The fact is that the mystery of the Church continues, in unfathomable depth, the mystery of Mary—the mystery of her Virginal Motherhood that is at once, by the quickening power of the Holy Spirit, sanctified and sanctifying.

Tradition enthusiastically refers to Mary as the model, the pattern of the Church, its point of origin and perfection in Christ. As Léon Bloy perceived, the Redemption was triumphant in her at its very onset. She is truly the "supereminent" member of the Church. For she is the Maiden "full of grace," "full of the Trinity," the "*Panagia*," the "world of intact, divinized humanity," the "eschatological icon of the Church" (Buoyer), its "seed and pleroma, its dawn and splendor," whose Assumption heralds the Church's triumph in the complete emergence of mankind redeemed and transfigured in Christ. Indeed, with the daring of faith we may even say (using an expression of Père Sertillanges, taken from another context) that Mary was the "Church before the Church." She was its prototype.

In the first place the Virgin Mary, *Virgo Fidelis*, is the type of the believing Church that welcomes God's Word. It was the faithful Virgin, the "culmination of all the aspirations, inspirations, graces, prefigurations which filled the Old Testament," the "epitome and incarnation of the long waiting of centuries" (Daniélou), who, "in the name of all humanity" (Aquinas), gave herself in total, utterly pure consecration to humanity's Bridegroom. Her *Amen* was the unconditional, unequivocal consent of all mankind and all creation to the Divine importunings. She, "holy and without blemish" (Eph. 5:27–28), conceived without sin, who had denied relationship to man, entered "in the role of the human race itself" (Pope Leo XIII), and in response to God's initiative, into the active abandonment and receptivity of bridal relationship with God:

"Behold the handmaid of the Lord; be it done to me according to thy word" (Lk. 1:38).

And so, "through a woman came foolishness, through a virgin wisdom" (St. Ambrose). "What the virgin Eve had tied up by unbelief, this the Virgin Mary loosened by faith," becoming "the advocate of the virgin Eve" and thus, as the human race fell into bondage to death through a virgin, so it is also rescued by a Virgin" (St. Irenaeus).

The Bridal-Virgin, the New Paradise of the Most High, whose presence the Gospels underscore at the progressive stages in the founding of the Church—the Incarnation, the Passion, and Pentecost—thus anticipated in her very essence the perfect, surpassing holiness of the Church.

Mary is also the living symbol of human cooperation in the actual work of Redemption. As the eminent Protestant theologian, Karl Barth, has perceived, Catholic faith regarding her Maternity sums up symbolically, in its special character, the doctrine of human cooperation in the Redemption, and provides the synthesis or matrix concept of the entire dogma of the Church. Her fiat was a cooperation from the very inception of the great task undertaken by the Word of God. He was enfleshed in her womb: his Body was made and shaped of Mary's flesh and blood. "She engendered God" (St. Ignatius the Martyr). And as Christ grew into manhood and eventually took leave of her to go and fulfill his Father's Plan, she continued to be solicitious for him. . . .

But Mary is also necessarily the care-full Mother of the members of her divine Son's Mystical Body. For in conceiving Christ physically, she conceived the Church, his Body (Eph. 1:23) mystically—and continues to be solicitous for its well-being. "The generation of Christ is the origin of the Christian people; for the birth of the Head is also the birth of the Body"

(St. Leo). "In the chaste womb of the Virgin, Christ took to himself flesh, and united to himself the spiritual Body formed of those who were to believe in him. Hence Mary, bearing the Savior within her, may also be said to have borne all of those whose life was contained in the life of the Savior . . . Hence, albeit in a spiritual and mystical fashion, we are all children of Mary; she is the Mother of us all . . ." (St. Pius X, *Ad Diem Illum*). And "can a woman forget her child? Let her forget; I will not be forgetful of thee" (Is. 49:15). She continues to be "the Mother of Life" (Gregory of Nyssa), the "pure womb which regenerates men unto God" (St. Irenaeus).

The astounding truth is that Mary, the Mediatrix in Christ between God and us, Our Lord's humble associate in the mysteries of Redemption, *Socia Passionis*, the companion of the Passion, continues to cooperate with the Holy Spirit, her Spouse, in the mission of the Word that is now being realized in the Church's apostolate. In her *Fiat*, and throughout her entire existence on earth, the New Eve acted on behalf of all humanity—and she continues this representative, intercessory role in the development of the life of Christ in her spiritual children. Just as it was her mysterious destiny to be present in Israel before her Son, fulfilling in her being and action the centuries-long Advent for the coming of the Messiah, and just as she then readied creation, filling every valley and bringing low every mountain and hill (Is. 40:3–5) for his coming, so she now continues to prepare for his subsequent comings, through the Church, into the hearts of individual persons and into entire cultures and nations. The reason is that Christ, though he has come among us, remains always the One who is to come (Ap. 1:4; 4:8), for his presence in history is not yet fully accomplished. His mystical incarnation within humanity remains an awesome process that advances to his Second Coming; and in the long interval between Pentecost and his

return, Mary—mankind's "youngest sister" (Bernanos)—
helps prepare us for that great moment, cooperating with the
Holy Spirit in his outpourings of grace on mankind, and in his
recreation of humanity from inside its depths. In a happy
analogy Jean Daniélou likens her to prevenient grace that pre-
disposes sinful man for the arrival of the One who is All-Holy.

It is understandable, therefore, that Mary is the maternal
figure of the Mother Church. "Just as the maternal function
of Mary is to give the God-Man to the world, so the maternal
function of the Church is to give us Christ" (Carl Feckes).
Thus St. Catherine of Arles invites us to compare these two
mothers: "The Spirit overshadowed Mary and his blessing
does the same to the Church at the baptismal fountain. Mary
conceived her Son without sin, and the Church destroys all sin
in those whom she regenerates. By Mary there was born he
who was at the beginning; by the Church is reborn he who
perished at the beginning. The first brought forth for many
peoples, the second brings forth these peoples. The one gave
us her Son, remaining a Virgin; through her Son, who is her
virgin Bridegroom, the other continually brings forth children. . . ." As Mary bore the earthly, physical Christ, the
Church bears the Eucharistic Christ. The parallels between
Mary and the Church are numerous, for both are mothers, in
different modes it is true, but both in virtue of true motherhood. And Mary's maternity is that which proceeded the other
as its promise and type.

Consequently, our apostolate, inserted in the Church of
which Mary is the prototype, is a cooperation with the Virgin-
Mother in her supernatural labor that will continue until the
Second Coming of her Son. It is a true participation in the
spiritual fruitfulness of her messianic motherhood.

If our apostolate must be ingrafted into the Church for its
very existence it must likewise be Marian. To envisage one

without the other would be monstrous—as though, in the actual unfolding of God's plan for mankind, Christ were conceivable apart from his immaculate Mother. "Mary without her Motherhood; a Christian without the apostolic spirit: the two resemble each other. Both alike are incomplete, lacking reality or substance, and would be a distortion of the divine plan" (Frank Duff).

Our salvation—all that we are and do, and therefore our apostolate—remains ever dependent on her consent in faith, and on the Child, Creator-creature, our Brother and Savior and Lord, that she bore. It was she who, under God, made the Incarnation possible. And she continues to care for the Mystical Body, the Church, "the Incarnation continued," with the same attention that she gave her Son during their lives in Palestine. Nazareth has now become the cosmos of the ages; and it is our duty and privilege to assist Mary in the prodigious work entrusted to her by the Almighty.

This demands that we be devoted to Our Lady—not, however, with the intermittent, weak, sentimentalized, counterfeit practice that calls down the reproaches of even the most friendly critics. Rather, it should be a strong interior union with Jesus through Mary, who is Mother through her charity and Virgin through her faith (St. Ambrose; Lk. 1:45; 11:27–28); and an active service in the spirit of the Maiden who, with the Divine Infant already within her womb, "arose and went with haste into the hill country" (Lk. 1:39) to help her cousin Elizabeth. To repeat: this is not maudlin excess, but a realizing in authentic faith (that comes from God only) the divine Will in our regard, and not attempting to set limits to Mary's unchangeable mediatory position in the Divine Plan. Mary's "yes" endures eternally, and to be united with her Son's being and action, we must plunge ourselves in the climate of this *Fiat;* we must unite our "yes" with hers.

Only when our apostolate is rooted in true, sober, warm devotion to Mary does it develop with a fullness and a balance that safeguards it from all deviations. Only when it is a participation in her spiritual fecundity do we, like St. Paul, beget others in Christ (Phil. 1:10).

This is why Mother Church repeatedly reminds us of the two great *"Ecces"* in Holy Scripture: *"Ecce Agnus Dei"* and *"Ecce Ancilla Domini,"*—"Behold the Lamb of God" and "Behold the handmaid of the Lord." For both point to the Mystery of the Word of God-become-Man by the will of his Father, and to our involvement, by the action of the Holy Spirit, in this Mystery.

Now, to advance in total engagement in this Mystery we must do precisely what God Himself did; *we must regard the humility of his handmaid* (Lk. 1:48), the humility that disarmed Divine Justice. And then, with the help of the Holy Spirit (upon whom Mary, mere creature, also depended), imitate her virtue, for it was our Lady's humility that opened her soul to the flood of grace and facilitated the accomplishment of God's all merciful designs. It was the rich soil in which all her other virtues took root and burgeoned.

We must remember that this is the peerless virtue that Christ recommended above all things, "Christianity's inmost secret," the unassuming strength that many of us, like Nietzsche, interpret as base weakness. Without this supernatural recognition and unaffected acknowledgment of our personal reality, our so-called apostolate soon degenerates (as the Legion of Mary handbook emphasizes) into a self-exaltation, a self-seeking, a self-sufficiency, a self-conceit, a self-love, a self-satisfaction, a self advancement, a self-will. As

Louis Mary de Montfort assures us, only by willingly submitting ourselves to Mary's guidance, consecrating ourselves to the gentle rule of this Queen who ceaselessly cooperates with the Spirit in the realization of the Church's mission, can we the more quickly and surely advance in holiness and thereby make true progress in our apostolate. For to be an apostle is to be ecclesial, is to be Marian!

Daniélou alerts us to the furrow that Our Lady sinks into the very substance of our twentieth-century history—as evidenced, for example, by the extraordinary apparitions just before the opening of our century and since; the official consecration of the universe to Mary Immaculate; the Marian Year; the definition of the dogma of the Assumption and the proclamation of the Queenship of Mary; the founding of more religious societies in honor of the Mother of God in this century than since the Church's beginnings; and the intense awakening of interest in Mariology. And he rightly would have us note the converging of this vast Marian movement with that of the Apostolate, a meeting that is "not accidentally, but brought about and willed as such by the Holy Spirit."

For where Mary is present, there is the Church, there is the Paraclete, her Divine Spouse, bestowing superabundance of grace. As never before in history, she is present among us of this era, preparing us for the New Pentecost as she once readied the Christians of the Upper Room (Acts 1).

Apostolate

15 * A Supernatural Work

*Neither he who plants is anything, nor he who waters,
but God who gives the growth.*

(1 Cor. 3:7)

*What would be the feelings of an authentic Catholic
at the sight of an apostle who sets up a claim, at least
implicitly, to do without God, to impart to souls even
the smallest degree of divine life?*

*"A madman!" he would exclaim on hearing an apostle
making use of such talk: "My God, do not raise an
obstacle to my enterprise, do not put a check on it,
and I will undertake to carry it through successfully."*

*God owes it to the humanity of his Son to put these
false christs to confusion, by paralyzing their works
of pride or by allowing them only to show like a
passing mirage.*

Dom. J. B. Chautard, O.C.R.

IT CANNOT BE too often emphasized that our apostolate,
the prolongation of Christ's mission, is essentially *supernatu-ral*. In the preaching of the Word, in the administration of
the sacraments, in the total liturgical action, indeed, in every
rhythm of its life, the Church recalls us to this paramount
truth.

St. Augustine, commenting on the cure of the paralytic at
the pool at Bethsaida, observed that Christ "moved the water
by his mere presence."

Our vocation, as Christ's apostles, is to be united with him
in his energizing presence, so that we may become, as Paul
Claudel put it, supernatural "centers of composition" in a
cosmos of men and things that has been shattered by sin.

But it is one we too easily forget; nor do we heed the Church's insistence. Repeatedly Satan confronts us with the third temptation with which he tried our Lord himself, baiting us with alluring opportunity to extend the Kingdom of Heaven (so he, the father of lies, claims), provided we worship him in the denial in practice of the reality of divine grace and of God.

Not infrequently the contemporary obsession with increasing demonic power over nature and even over persons infiltrates our Christian perspective and perverts our apostolate. The vast dimensions of our mission fires us with enthusiasm, but we lack the holy patience that is born of the profound, strong virtues of humility, poverty, and hope. We are impatient that the Church outstrip the World; we are satisfied only with results that are immediate and tangible, triumphs that enhance a power that, in pitiful self-delusion, we attribute to Christ. Sacraments and the like are paraded: this gives the mimicry some prestige; but actually they are degraded to a form of magicism, for the "bolus of our apostolate" depends on human techniques, adaptations, compromise. The whole, imbecile, cut-rate business is geared to Success; *it is not Christian apostolate.*

It is interesting that such efforts very often meet with apparent gains for the Church that impress enormously. But the monument quickly disintegrates from within: its empty claim to be an extension of God's Kingdom from the beginning dooms it to frustration. Instead of a mighty edifice (symbolized, I daresay, by reinforced concrete!), we are left with a dung heap and the edge of despair.

There is one terrifying aspect to all this: the fact that the "apostolate" that is not united intrinsically with the Mystical Body of Christ contributes material to the satanic "body" that incorporates all the evil will of humanity and Hell. Its very essence is the caricature of supernatural reality—the stuff of which the diabolical is made.

It is, therefore, of capital importance that we recall to mind, day-in and day-out, that our apostolate—our share in Christ's mission that is continued in his Church—must be a work that is begun and developed in the vast, fresh perspectives of supernatural, triumphant faith (Jn. 5:4–5). As St. John tirelessly repeated (2 Jn. 1:4; 3 Jn. 1:4) we must walk in the truth—which, St. Paul emphasized, is to walk by the Spirit (Gal. 5:25). Having encountered Christ in his sacraments and revelation, and having been sanctified in him (1 Cor. 1:2), and now daily advancing in union with him (2 Cor. 16:7), we stake our entire lives in the power of his word (Rom. 1:15). He takes the initiative (1 Jn. 4:10) and we follow him (Lk. 9:23). We adhere to his person, engaging our total being, not simply in principles and doctrines, but in the strong, deliberate doing of his truth (Jn. 3:21)—the Christian confrontation, as Mounier calls it. And in practicing the truth, we move deeper into the existential experience of the things of God and become increasingly illumined by his light (Jn. 3:21), so that our thought reflects that of Christ himself (1 Cor. 2:16). Thus we strive all the more eagerly to witness to the Word of Life (1 Jn. 1:1) among others; we become epiphanies, bearers of truth (Is. 52:7), fellow workers for the truth (3 Jn. 1:8). Like Mary and Abraham, the great believers, we leave the cramped dimensions of the merely human (the self-righteous cliques of not a few Catholic organizations!), and progressively enter into the freedom of God's designs! (Jn. 8:31–32).

Similarly, we must remember that to be sanctified in the truth (Jn. 17:17), we must practise it in charity (Eph. 4:15).

As Péguy bluntly remarked in reference to the frequent penury of so-called apostolic efforts, "It is not arguments that are lacking, but charity."

This is the charity that is poured into our hearts by the Holy Spirit (Rom. 5:5): the "bond of perfection" (Col. 3:14); the "fulfilling of the Law" (Rom. 13:10). It is at once the sap and the climate of the apostolate, without which growth remains utterly impossible.

The terrifying ennui in which we sometimes find ourselves is due particularly to our preoccupation with "apostolate" that is replete with hackneyed bric-a-brac of words and actions that have been squeezed dry of supernatural love of God and man. It is only by God's grace that we are jolted into awareness of ourselves as purveyors of eviscerated platitudes.

But, having been baptized into Christ and having "put on Christ" (Gal. 3:27), our temporal-eternal destiny is to exult in the new love that wells up from the depths of our remade being. Ours is the magnificent prerogative to love with the love with which God himself loves: to love him with our total existence (Mt. 22:35–40), with a love as "strong as death" (Cant. 8:6); and to love our neighbor—never a "superfluous," replaceable human!—as Christ our Redeemer loves us (Jn. 12:15; 13:34); even to the supreme self-sacrifice (34–35). This is the "Royal Law" (Jas. 2:8). Nor is this charity a matter of vague ideals, but one to be lived in concrete, immediate human context, incarnated in the grit of day-to-day living.

We must further realize that authentic apostolate is buoyed up by a supernatural hope in God that is never confounded (Ps. 30:2), that never disappoints (Rom. 5:3–5). This is the enduring hope in our divine Lord (1 Thes. 1:3). As disciples of Christ, our glory is in his Cross (Gal. 6:14): our extraordinary mission is to make sure that his Cross be not made void among men (1 Cor. 1:17). So we must happily expect to be nailed with him on the cross of our apostolate's obstacles and burdens.

We must remember that God's grace is always sufficient for us, and that we are powerful in our actual weakness when we lean on the strength of the Almighty (2 Cor. 12:9–10).

This is no facile optimism, depending on human ingenuity and "strokes of luck," but a realism rooted in a trust that is upheld by the divine assurance of absolute victory (Jn. 16:33). Apart from this supernatural hope, to undertake the apostolate would be sheer madness.

To repeat, then: our apostolate, a participation in that of the Church, is essentially the communication of divine life, a divine work. Without assiduous union with Christ, apart from whom we can accomplish nothing (Jn. 15:5), authentic apostolate is absolutely impossible. Certainly, human resources must be employed at the service of the apostolate, but only with the understanding of their impotency unless God's grace be present and active. The true apostolate is always united with the divine source of sanctity, so that its deepening and broadening consists fundamentally less in agitation and more and more in radiation of virtue throughout the fabric of human existence. In other words, the call to involvement in the Church's apostolate is at the same time a challenge to vitalize further our interior life in Christ communicated through his Church: *growth in holiness is indispensable to development of our apostolate.*

Relative to our task, isn't this the great lesson that emerges from the Old and New Testaments: that through our poverty, humbly recognized, God's supernatural power will burst forth?

16 * Redemptive Incarnation

> *Mutual human availability is possible only in and through man's bodiliness. . . . It is as Man that the Son is the Mediator of grace; He is Mediator in his Humanity, according to the ways of humanity. His human mediation of grace, therefore, presupposes his corporeality. Redemption turns its face towards us in Christ's glorified bodiliness . . ."*
>
> E. Schillebeeckx, O.P.

> *And the Word was made flesh, and dwelt among us.*
> (John 1:14)

> *The Incarnation is the first stage of a process that is to reach fulfillment in the Transfiguration, that is, in the penetration of the world by the light of Christ. If we tarry too long on the first stage, the process will remain incomplete. In Christ we find both movements. He became Man, and fully Man, but in order to make us gods. Without the second part, the first would make no sense whatever.*
>
> Jean Daniélou

OUR APOSTOLATE must be an *ascending, redemptive incarnation*.

The action indicated here demands sober, prayerful study. Far too many have projected into the terms "incarnate apostolate" their own itch for an oscillating relativism that is completely alien to true Christian activity. Instead of being won over by their factitious compromises, we must look to the models provided us in Christ and his Church and thereby deepen our insight into the intrinsic structural dynamic of our apostolate.

For, strictly speaking, there is only one Apostolate—the Mission of the Only Begotten Son whom the Father sent to redeem and divinize a fallen mankind by the communication of divine life. This tremendous undertaking of the Word, the profound mystery hidden in the eternal silence and now revealed in these last days, is the source of all apostolate: apart from it there is only caricature and barren dispersal.

Now, in the accomplishment of the mission of the Son of God two stages or movements, if we may so describe them, are discernible, the second the fulfillment of the first. Initially was realized the descent (called by the Greeks the *katabasis*) of the Word into the human condition, the integral incarnation wherein the Son, in sacredly awesome annihilation (*kenosis*) of divine splendor, assumed authentic human nature, *absque peccato*, except sin. The Word became flesh (*soma*), that is, the Word embraced the values and vulnerability of fallen human nature and "lived among us" (Jn. 1:14): Christ, "God's Sacrament," submitted to the lot of mankind in the complex fabric of history.

But, the Fathers hasten to remind us, if God became man it was in order that man might become divinized by a participation in God's own nature. There is the second stage in the mission of the Son of God, the ascending movement (*anabasis*) that culminates the Incarnation of the Word by the transfiguration of mankind—and through mankind the entire cosmos—by the glorified humanity of the Risen Lord. The Word assumed human nature in order to transform it: to divorce this aim (directed to the external glory of God) from the total reality of the Incarnation is to render it incoherent.

Turning to the Church we find the same two-fold movement inherent to its advance, for the Church, "Sacrament of Christ," his "permanent incarnation," necessarily continues his divinizing action. Through the Church, the deifying action of the Incarnate Word permeates man and the world in which man is actual—the remotest ramifications of cultures and epochs that are fashioned in and by him. Generation after generation, century by century, the Church makes Christ present, incorporating all human values to effect their redemptive transformation and, in turn, to prolong Christ's very incarnation through them.

The Church's action is never limited to a movement of incarnation—destroying Christianity in an anthropology, as Comte and his like would have it. It is never immobilized by identification with the human condition of any period or geography; it remains transcendent, descending into the mud of man's history only to transfigure him in the effulgence of the Risen Lord.

Here is a profound truth, of far-reaching consequences, that we must grasp and live: that the structural dynamic of our apostolate in all its phases must embody the twofold movement inherent in the mission of Christ in His Mystical Body. It must be incarnated in the living flesh of the idiom of our time—in all its realities, even though weak and groping, never in its sin—but all the while impregnating it with the divine energy, and contributing it purified and transfigured unto the building up of the Church.

Two temptations, consequently, are to be carefully avoided. First, there is the imprudent, overriding anxiety to incarnate our apostolate in the "Spirit of the Age" and to abandon its transcendent nature, resulting in a feverish proliferation of merely human projects that eventually petrify and disintegrate. On the other hand, there is the disregard, apathetic or even militant, for the truth that the Church, as a living organism, "lives by virtue of its 'response' to the environment in which it has been placed by the Creator" (Father Thornton), and a refusal to incarnate Christianity in the authentic values of our age, an "angelism" that undermines the profound meaning of the Incarnation.

Concerning the movement of incarnation specifically, we must remember that by his becoming flesh the Word of God entered into communion with the total reality of human nature, as well as with every individual human person. He assumed every potential good in man's being, every intellectual, volitional and emotional value in human nature. Simultaneously, the love of the God-become-Man reached out to all mankind, to all persons irrespective of their physical characteristics, their talents, and their social status.

As with Christ, so with his Mystical Body. The "dynamic universality of the Church's principles of unity" reaches out "to assimilate, fill, win over to God, reunite and bring to perfection in Christ, the whole man and all men. . . . Every human value can be 'recapitulated' in Christ, that is to say revivified by his Spirit, and taken up into the unity of his Body, which is the Church . . . and become mystically (pneumatically), as it were, the flesh and members of the new Adam. Christ will not be complete till he has, in this way, incorporated the whole man in each of us, and all human values lying scattered in all their variety throughout the world. For he has—and so has the Church, his Body—the capacity to bring all this together in himself unto God" (Yves Congar).

The Christian apostle, united intimately by grace with this inherent dynamism of the Church, is by vocation—both duty and privilege—a "universal brother," bearer of the title that stirred the passionate spirit of Charles de Foucald.

Though necessarily fashioned in personality by a particular environment, national, cultural, social and economic, he strives to rise beyond this limited complex of reactions to real-

ity, so that he may become attuned to and appreciate all
human values, including, with special emphasis, those revealed
by reaction to contemporary events. This, of course, does not
imply that he must rid himself of his "native" orientation.
Quite the contrary. Christ, our model, always remained a loyal
Jew. Without ancestral orientation one becomes neutralized
in personality, and has nothing original and organic left to
contribute to mankind of the Church. It means that the
apostle must not allow the spiritual mold in which he was
formed to crush his expansion of soul; and that he must sincerely endeavor to open his natively enriched personality to all
the wealth of man's spiritual dimensions, and assimilate of
their plenitude.

This is no easy task! It demands constant self-renunciation,
for ingrained prejudices militate against this maturation of
spirit. It never ceases: the human horizons are infinite; they
open on to the very immensity of God. And it is a most delicate work, challenging the apostle to enter, with redeeming,
respectful love, into communication with his fellow men
(which necessitates that he learn to translate the Christian
message into contemporary idiom), and into communion with
the cosmos of powerful matter (including his own flesh) that
is presently being uncovered to his wonder.

All this may be called a "Christian," "vertical" universality,
embracing the heights and depths of man himself and his
values. There is also the Christian "horizontal," geographic
universality, the Church's dynamic, and therefore the apostle's, that encircles in welcome all mankind of every time and
place.

The apostle usually lives most of his Christian life of prayer
and action within his parish. It is especially in the parish that
the Church becomes actualized, becoming "an actual event in

place-time apprehensibility." There it acts in fuller sacramental, historical measure. It is in the "placeness" of the parish that the apostle encounters (above all, in the community Mass) the localized concretion of God's salvivic will. From within the *ecclesia* of his parish he advances in interior holiness and labors in the Church's apostolate.

But while the apostle holds a singular relationship to his parish, and is responsible in a very special manner to all who dwell within its bounds—not only his Catholic brethren, but non-Catholics as well—his Christian vision and aspiration and, depending on many circumstances, his action, transcend boundaries and extend to all mankind.

In sum, the apostle must embody the universalism of the Incarnation in all his being and activity.

In concert with this apostolic dynamism of incarnation there must always be a corresponding movement of spiritual ascent. All man and all men, and through mankind all creation, must be restored and thereby transformed in Christ.

It is by advancing in the likeness of Christ that the apostle can fulfill this facet of his mission. By becoming more Christlike, through cooperation with the inspirations of the Holy Spirit, by encounter with Jesus in the sacraments, and through communion with him in prayer, the apostle shares in the very power of Christ, whereby he draws all mankind and the cosmos to himself on high in glory. It is not merely a matter of lifting him aloft as did Moses the brazen serpent (Nm. 21:9), when we are united to his humanity in holiness, it is he who lives in us (Gal. 3:20), and transfuses our entire being with his energizing virtue. Upheld by his Spirit, we ourselves actually become centers of integrating attraction, through whom Christ draws the whole man and all men into the supernatural plane of participation in the Divine Nature.

Thus, rooted in the time-place humility of the Incarnation, our apostolate moves to the eternal, transfigured glory of the Ascension. This constitutes its inner dynamism.

17 ✳ A Sacramental Work

God has always remained faithful to his own methods of teaching us salvation. Because God loves man and has a soverign respect for our earthbound humanity— for our reality as persons who in their own bodiliness live in a world of people and of things, and thereby grow to spiritual maturity—God always offers us the kingdom of Heaven in an earthly guise. So he did in the Old Testament. So it was in the ephapax: *the appearance once and for all of God the Redeemer in human shape. So, too, finally, does he continue to* **teach us in the Sacramental Church, which is the visi**ble *organ on earth of the living Lord.*

E. Schillebeeckx, O.P.

I meet you, O Christ, in your Sacraments.
St. Ambrose

B‌y focusing our attention on the sacramental character of our apostolate, we shall deepen our appreciation for its total dimension—the twofold movement of incarnation-transfiguration previously discussed—and avoid circumscribing it after the manner of heretical extremes, perpetually recurrent temptations.

We have already established the truth that apostolate is possible only through insertion within the supernatural organic structure of the Mystical Body of Christ, a union that determines its very existence and apart from which obtains only baneful imposture.

This insertion in the Church is an intimate, unique identification with the Great Sacrament of Christ that continues his epiphany and operation among men. By it we are taken up into the movement of Christ and his Church, *a movement that is in essence sacramental.*

Christ, the God-Man, is the tremendous Sacrament of God. He is the all-holy Shekinah, the tangible presence of the hidden divinity; the Sign in whose concrete, historical humanity God himself was manifested; his palpable visitation among men. In the mystery of Jesus, Father Gustave Weigel observes, "God in love transcended his transcendence," an outward sign signifying a divine approach in benevolence.

The Church, the God-Man mystically continued, is the Sacrament, the universal symbol, of Christ, that makes him operatively present in time and space. And, because the Church prolongs the redemptive Incarnation of the Word by the "sacramental diffusion of supernatural life into humanity, in all its temporal breadth," it is necessarily, of its very essence, a sacramental organism, constituted by sacraments, living and growing and working through sacraments. Every aspect of its being and activity is sacramental, divine and human, transcendent and empirical, an ascending incarnation that returns man, transformed in the resurrection of Christ, to God.

Unquestionably, if our apostolate is to be authentic it too must be sacramental; and it can be such only by being vitalized by the sacramental reality of the organism, the "community of sacraments," which is the Church.

During recent centuries the Church's sacraments, and thereby also the sacramentals, "satellites" of the sacraments, have very often been reduced to a mutilated, mechanistic, utilitarian conception—bluntly described by Bayart as a reduction of the sacraments to a kind of authorized application of patent (supernatural) medicine, capsules of grace. Today's remarkable awakening of interest in the Liturgy is correcting this distortion, one of the many unhappy by-products spawned by the Protestant Revolt. Meditative study, rooted in the living tradition of the Church, is resulting in a deeper appreciation of the decisive significance of sacred symbol, of the meaning of sacraments as signs of faith of the whole Church as well as of the individual, of their import as instrumental causes of grace, and above all, of their reality as activities of the Risen Christ, who is today and forever (Heb. 13:8). Noteworthy is the fact that this sacramental revival coincides with the contemporary upsurge of Catholic Action.

The profound truth—underscored by St. Thomas Aquinas, but unfortunately neglected—is that the Church not only applies the redemptive acts of Christ; through the sacraments the Church *continues* to realize and extend them in history. Through the reception of the sacraments we encounter Christ in his Church, and he assimilates us to his life, to his Incarnation, Passion, Resurrection, Ascension, the total complex of his physical, historical activity; and, according to our faith and devotion, *his Life receives new actuality in us*. This is why St. Leo was able to write that "whatever was evident in the life of Christ has passed over into the sacraments"—and, through these sacred symbols, to us his members.

The sacraments, then, are the mysterious signs, prefigured in the wonders of the Old Testament, that anticipate and embody the future realities of eternity in God; because, through the Mystical Body, they insert us into Christ's mysteries, conforming us more and more to his likeness in being and in action. Through the sacraments, Origen insists, Christ's mysteries are fulfilled in and through us. For, by becoming increasingly configured to Christ, our presence and our activity become, in a very real sense, sacramental—not only signs that witness to God, but signs that are invested with the supernatural influence indicated by Christ when He tells us that we must be the leaven (Mk. 9:48–49), the salt (Lk. 13:20–21), the light (Mt. 5:15) that will cooperate with the Spirit in the renewal of humanity and the cosmos.

But we must always bear in mind that the sacramental character of the Church is not confined to the sacraments as such, but overflows from these sacramental concentrations into all the dimensions of its life. As Karl Rahner rightly insists, in objection to religious monomania that would stultify the liberty of the Spirit, God "has bound us to the sacraments, but he has not bound himself and his grace to the sacraments." While the seven sacraments, particularly the incomparable Sacrament of the Eucharist, are the established means of vital encounter with Christ, the Holy Spirit works to employ every facet of human existence in like sacramental manner.

We may therefore regard our apostolate as a cooperation with the Paraclete in the sacramentalizing of our very being and our activity, so that through us and our actions—now signs of the Divine Presence and activity—mankind meets with Christ. In us he becomes mystically "corporified" (Mohler).

18 * Christ's Return

> *Rejoice in the Lord always; again I say, rejoice! The Lord is near. Have no anxiety.*
>
> (Phil. 4:4–6)

Every instant is eschatological.

H. Butterfield

The eschatological is not something simply absent from the present, any more than what is transcendent is exterior to everyday reality; on the contrary, it is the foundation of the present and the term of its movement—it is the marrow of the present, as it were, and exercises over it a hidden power.

Henri de Lubac, S.J.

Our apostolate must be viewed within the magnificent perspectives of the Second Coming of Christ; otherwise its forward dynamism, its élan, and its patient expectancy, are incomprehensible.

Here we turn to the ubiquitous Christian paradox: the emergence of life in death, of renewal in disintegration. We are called to cooperate with the Almighty in the realization of his great work on earth, yet at the same time we are aware that this world is passing (1 Cor. 7:31), that it is gradually being superseded, rendered obsolete!

The fact is that we are involved in the Paschal mystery that embraces all mankind, all creation. In his Resurrection, anticipated momentarily in the luminous splendor of the Transfiguration on Mount Tabor, the Lord irreversibly (the Greek *hapax*) inaugurated a new order of existence for humanity, and through humanity for the entire cosmos. We are risen (Col. 2:12) in Christ, whose humanity is eternally united with the divinity, and who now, at the right hand of the Father (Eph. 1:20), intervenes for us (Heb. 9), and fills all creation with his presence (Eph. 4:10), attracting all mankind —and through humanity the entire cosmos to himself (Jn. 12:32). Already we are sons of God (1 Jn. 3:2), and even now, through the sacramental organism of the Church, a new heaven and a new earth—the *novissimus,* the new creation beyond history—are not only prefigured but are in essence achieved within the deeps of the cosmos. The eternal Easter has already begun. A new order of being, on the level of the Risen Christ, is gradually penetrating our present existence; and we, who are baptized in Christ, must associate ourselves with this new creation, and cooperate in its transforming penetration of our contemporary universe of men and things.

But this divinizing juvenescence of all created being, that had been degraded in Adam's sin, remains hidden and incomplete. It even seems that "all things continue as they were from the beginning of creation" (2 Pt. 3:4).

The fact is that, while our citizenship is already in heaven (Phil. 3:20), and "we know that, when he appears, we shall be like to him, for we shall see him just as he is" (1 Jn. 3:2), "it has not yet appeared what we shall be" (3:4). While we confidently look forward to the apocalyptic dissolution of all creation (2 Pt. 3:11) from which shall emerge "new heavens and a new earth, according to his promises," we know that Christ's Mystical Body remains incomplete in stature, that his kingdom is not yet established in its entirety.

Therefore, this short time (1 Cor. 7:29-31) in which we live—the period between the Ascension of our Lord and his Second Return—is one of urgent expectancy (Mt. 24:42). Even sub-human creation moves with mysterious groaning toward the great Day of the Lord (Rom. 8:22).

It is a time when the patience of God waits (1 Pt. 3:20). God has already judged the world (Ap. 14:7), but he has granted us a respite; for he is "long-suffering, not wishing that anyone should perish, but that all should turn to repentance (2 Pt. 3:9). On his return the Son of Man will judge all peoples (Mt. 25:31-32). Meanwhile, we have opportunity to unite ourselves with the remnant (Rom. 11:5) on the Bark of Peter, who, like Noah and his family, can brave the floods of divine judgment (Gn. 7, ff.; Dt. 8:2–4).

This period of postponement and decision is a "little while" (Jn. 16:16), a delay (*mora*) that spans the centuries, for "one day with the Lord is as a thousand years" (2 Pt. 3:8). We cannot know the exact moment of Christ's return. Not even the angels know it (Mk. 13:32; Acts 1:7). Therefore we must await in vigilant readiness (Mt. 25:12), and govern our whole lives by the hope of his glorious return (Ti. 2:13).

Obviously, it is a time of crucial probation, of disciplining chastisements and crises, whereby God proves the dispositions of men's hearts (Dt. 8:2–4). Such trials were already prefigured in the journey of the Hebrews in the wilderness (Nm. 14:34). They are hard, but, then, "the sufferings of the present time are not worthy to be compared with the glory to come, that will be revealed in us" (Rom. 8:18).

And it is a time for ever-advancing apostolate of the Church militant. As may be gathered from what we have already outlined, Almighty God has withheld the Parousia of his beloved Son until the evangelization of all peoples is completed. "The Gospel of the Kingdom shall be preached in the whole world for a testimony of all nations, and then shall the consummation come" (Mt. 24:8–14). "It is not for you to know the time or moments which the Father hath put in his own power: but you shall receive the power of the Holy Ghost coming upon you, and you shall be witnesses unto me in Jerusalem, and in all Judea, and even to the uttermost part of the earth" (Acts 1:6–8). The collective fulfillment of the work of the apostolate is the providential, indispensable condition for the Second Return of Christ—and, to a very special extent, the preaching of the Gospel; for the white rider and steed, the Word of God, must first encircle the globe, before the advent of the other three riders and horses, who will bring with them the hell of war and famine and destruction and death to all mankind (Ap. 6:1–8; 19:11–13).

And there is also the singular mystery of Judaism. "A partial blindness only has befallen Israel," St. Paul wrote with sad, proud love for his Hebrew brethren (Rom. 11:25). Actually, "by their offense salvation has come to the Gentiles" (Rom. 11:11–12), according to the unfathomable designs of God, who can draw good out of historical events that were originally directed against his will. But after the collective evangelization of the Gentiles—also a mystery of grace (Eph. 3:1–6)—Israel will be converted and grafted onto the vine who is Christ (Rom. 11:25–26).

This, then, is the amazing truth, the significance of which we must endeavor to understand more fully: that we must *hasten* (Rom. 3:11–12) the final Advent of Christ. By very definition we Catholics are those who look forward with love to the Second Coming of Our Lord (2 Tm. 3:8). It is a love that is active, eagerly advancing his return by participating with zeal in the Church's apostolate. "It is still today" (Heb. 3:13). A teeming multitude await the preaching of the Gospel and the offer of supernatural life. There is yet time for them to encounter the Savior, to know and love him, and through him to know and love the blessed Trinity.

The exigencies of our apostolate, therefore, demand that it be eschatological—basically because supernatural love, the consuming motivation of our apostolate, presses us forward in unshakable, urgent, patient hope to the arrival of our Divine Bridegroom.

The true apostle is, indeed, a lover whose whole life has a lilt to its daily rhythm. *"Amen! Veni Domine Jesu!"* (Ap. 22:20). "Come, Lord Jesus!"

19 ✳ Ecclesial Obedience

> *And he went down with them, and came to Nazareth,*
> *and was subject to them; and his mother kept all these*
> *things carefully in her heart. And Jesus advanced in*
> *wisdom and age and grace before God and men.*
>
> (Lk. 2:51–52)

> *You, brethren, have been called unto liberty!*
>
> (Gal. 5:13)

> *Obedience is a virtue, truly necessary, but it is not*
> *a pure perfection. For it is a perfection only in crea-*
> *tures. God is free; he is not obedient. Christ was*
> *obedient, but in his human nature. Since, therefore,*
> *obedience is itself a perfection inferior to liberty, the*
> *incursions of obedience and so of authority into the*
> *realm of liberty ought not to be carried out without a*
> *proportionate cause.*
>
> Fr. Joseph Buckley (Marist)

Persistently interwoven into a maze of activity of our apostolate is the lurking possibility of equivocation. There is always the tendency to self-orientation, of espousing means and aims other than those determined by the exigencies of Christ's mission, of ultimately—under the guise of orthodoxy —announcing a Gospel of this world and promoting a salvation of man by man.

How, then, can we ascertain the validity of our engagement as apostolate?

The great criteria was repeatedly emphasized by St. Augustine: *it is the Church, the Great Sacrament of Universal Salvation, that alone guarantees our apostolate.* For where the Church is present and active, Christ is present and active. The insertion of our activity in the vital perspectives and rhythm of Christ's Mystical Body determines its very being as a participation in his divine mission. To quote Louis Lochet: "There are no apostles except through the Church and for the Church." "Apostolate" outside the Church can only result in a futile anarchical agitation that eventually de-divinizes and disperses.

Now, insertion in the Church means insertion into its hierarchical vitalizing dimensions. *Ubi Petrus, ibi Ecclesia!* The Church evolves within the fabric of its visible hierarchical authority; and our identity as living members of Christ is determined by our submission to this divinely constituted order.

To interpret this obedience as an unworthy servility to an intolerable tyranny is arrant nonsense. Essentially it is an interior submission to Christ in those who are invested with legitimate authority as his representatives. It is an unflagging trust in the Spirit whom Christ has sent, in the One who advances the Church notwithstanding the weaknesses, pretensions and vulgarities of men; in other words, it is a filial obedience to divine providence.

This deep attachment to the Christ in his Church, expressed and fulfilled through active submission to the mystery of visible hierarchical order (the great Cardinal Suhard called it the "Mysticism of the Hierarchy") guarantees our apostolate from all deception, quickening it with the true freedom of supernatural action and strengthening it in the infallible security of Divine Wisdom.

But more: the Church, "House of Obedience" (Origen) is ever solicitous that we ourselves be purified through our apostolate—which is an extension of our interior life. The renunciation of argumentative attitudes, the sacrifice of our own projects, the eager willingness to be guided by the Church, all provide a constant purification, a Cross, a sharing in the total self-annihilation of our divine lord (Heb. 5:8) who was obedient even to a death of consummate humiliation.

The realization of the social and personal spiritual fruitfulness of this "ecclesiastic" obedience is absolutely indispensable to the development of our Christian life. Its absence spells dismal failure.

It must be reiterated that this ecclesial obedience is poles apart from ignoble passivity to an ecclesiatical totalitarianism. The Catholic Church, in the manner of Christ its founder, reverences the supernaturally elevated spiritual-personal, individual uniqueness of its members. As a matter of fact, it is within its solidarity, reflecting the community of the most radical individuality of the blessed Trinity, that the Holy Spirit develops the full liberty that is their inalienable right as children of God. The Church recognizes the unexchangeable, unique responsibility of every single one of its members—a responsibility through whose successive fulfillment in innumerable free actions they decide their choice of eternal destiny. The Church cannot unburden its members of the initiative of this responsibility; though it is undeniable that in practice some bureaucratic ecclesiastics do their level best to attempt to do so, and often receive willing, submissive cooperation from laymen who wish to be free from the burden of their selves— the selves that make decisions.

Indeed, as Karl Rahner, S.J., has written in his excellent essay, "The Individual in the Church": "In every man there is a sphere of personal individuality, elevated by grace, which we may call 'private,' and which cannot and may not be governed and regimented by the Church in its reality as a visible, hierarchical, law-imposing society. This metaphysical level of man's being (conceptually, not really, distinct from his totality) is immediately open to the inspirations and impulses that the Holy Spirit directs to him *alone*—graces that may be apprehended by the gift traditionally called the 'discernment of spirits.' When the individual Christian responds to these movements of grace, his private religious life radiates itself in charismatic action; and this is tantamount to an expression of his unique vocation as an individual member of Christ's Mystical Body."

But while this private sphere of the Christian's personal individuality is *above* the Church's immediate juridical authority, it is emphatically not contrary to it. It is not a "sphere of arbitrary choices and of freedom from moral obligations to God." Quite the contrary. It is still another instance of the Christian paradox; for, at once, it is the focus of richer freedom in personal initiative, and more intense obedience to the imperative of God's call—an obedience that is further manifested in the individual's deeper and more alert loyalty to the authority of the Church. Its liberty is that of the children of God (Gal. 4:31), deriving its inherently untrammelled movement from adherence to the Divine Will.

Actually, what we confront in this brief meditation is the mystery of obedience in Christ; more specifically, the mystery of Nazareth that haunted the soul of Charles de Foucald.

The extraordinary obedience of Our Lord in Nazareth (Lk. 2:51–52) was the prelude (wastefully long, it would seem by human estimates) to his public ministry. Christ knew that he was the one Mediator between God and mankind (1 Tm. 2:5), the One commissioned to bring them abundant life (Jn. 10:10). And in this small segment of humanity, not only did he "elbow" his brethren, he espoused their existential, human condition. Plunged into its complexity, he was intimately aware of their misery and agony. There is no doubting whatsoever that his love for them constantly propelled his whole being towards the inauguration of his public ministry there and then. Notwithstanding, he adhered to the will of his Father, and restrained the holy zeal that scalded every fiber of his human make-up; and he persisted in hidden, redemptive, obedient presence among them. His "obedience unto death" (Phil. 2:8) was already realized in this amazing, deliberate "death" to his public ministry.

Now, unless we configure ourselves to Christ in his mystery of obedience; unless we obey the Paraclete who guides us, not only within the "private" sphere of our individuality, but from within the visible institution of Christ's Church, then our apostolate is vain. The most it will produce is disunity, a chaos begotten by pride.

20 ✳ Prayer

Pray without ceasing. In all things give thanks; for this is the will of God in Christ Jesus regarding you all.

(1 Thess. 5:17–18)

The most pressing duty of Christians is to live the liturgical life, and increase and cherish its supernatural spirit.

Pius XII

OUR EVALUATION of prayer, particularly in practice, all too frequently lacks robust, Christian proportions.

Not a few of us mistakenly treat prayer as at best a source of vitalizing grace that needs to be injected periodically into our daily routine of projects. Bluntly stated, this attitude defines prayer only in terms of apostolic exigencies, an irreplaceable refueling of supernatural help; and our consideration stops there. The result is that prayer so ordered eventually becomes a series of pragmatic exercises, concerned more with ideas than with Christ's mysteries, flat and banal, lacking in the full dimensions of true contemplative orientation. Instead of being directed in essence to the divinity, its movement rotates around our own activity which, ironically, soon becomes impoverished of supernatural élan and degenerates into a buzz of preoccupations. Even the exercise of prayer itself becomes part of the over-riding agitation.

Certainly the value and the necessity of the conscious exercise of prayer must not be minimized. It is the repeated turning of the whole human personality to God that gradually leads to the "spirit of prayer." Without its discipline the freedom of the spirit of prayer cannot be attained.

But it is precisely the latter that we undervalue, despite our Lord's insistent reminder that we must pray at all times (Lk. 10:10). Our prayer may not be limited to occasional acts—indispensable though they be—but should be the very condition, the all-pervasive climate, of our being and action. It must be the rhythm of our Christian life, a spiritual inhaling and exhaling in the divine presence, that the scheduled exercise of prayer presupposes and nourishes.

Nor, at the cost of absurd presumption and empty activism, may we neglect prayer in relation to our activity. It is the "very soul of the apostolate." Unless our action be prayer-full it cannot be apostolic: supernaturally it remains barren, a mere surface. Prayer illumines and supports effective apostolate, pervading our attempts with the love that derives from its mutual presence and immanence.

But, again, this far from exhausts the meaning of prayer.

For its basic urgency is aimed at glory of the Triune God. All authentic prayer, including "prayer of petition," is in essence adoration of the One who is consuming purity, the all-holy Being who has become our neighbor in the undiminished humanity of Christ. While rooted in our concrete history, with its innumerable burdens, through genuine prayer we transcend ourselves in the disposition to worship ("Hallowed be thy name"), humbly, confidently, bringing in this adoration our pressing needs ("Give us this day . . ."). Always the central dynamic of true prayer consists in divine praise.

The fact is that prayer, even in its summits, is itself apostolic. For the impulse of love, the content of prayer, reaches out to bring others to glorify the Love who is infinitely resplendent. Prayer is turned to God; but, though solitary, it brings within itself all creation. Similarly, our activity does not stop short with mankind: within itself it brings God to man and is oriented in and beyond man to the Almighty. In other words, prayer and apostolate are not two exclusive, opposing currents, rather, they reinforce each other and advance toward their one fulfillment in God through Christ.

We must not make the mistake of reducing prayer to the one dimension of a soliloquy, a human cry without a divine response. Prayer is a mutual communication between God and man; indeed, it is a participation in the profound dialogue between Christ and his eternal Father wherein our efforts discover their origin and completion, their silence and utterance. For in prayer, as in apostolate, the Son of God-become-Man is our prototype and our strength. Christ's entire life was centered on the accomplishment of the mission entrusted to him by his Father; but it was never for a moment an activity divorced from prayer. Our Lord's humanity, substantially united to the divinity, moved without interruption in the intimate presence of the Almighty; again and again he turned to the exercise of prayer, either in the communal liturgy of the Temple or in the solitude of the night and mountain. Always Christ's activity was shot through with contemplation.

In participating in the prayer-mission of Christ we co-operate, in a unique manner, in the Son's outpouring of love to his Father. Beholden to the Father in all things, yet equal to the Father in unity of nature, the Son cannot express his ineffable attachment by a self-dispossessing on the divine plane. But on the level of the Incarnation, having assumed an intact human nature in our alienated, dependent, existential condition, the Second Divine Person of the Trinity was able to surrender himself to his Father in sacrificial prayer and action. Within a created expression of his origin from and return to the Father (Jn. 16:28; Lk. 23:36), the Son of God revealed his unfathomable love in a human mode, a supreme worship that was accepted by the Father who, in turn, returned infinite love (Jn. 15:19). And in this divine dialogue our prayer (as well as its effusion in apostolate) is assumed and transfigured, our human cries take on the splendor of Christ's tremendous love.

It is by our insertion into the Church that we become partakers of Christ (Heb. 3:14) and thereby integrated into the perfect prayer. For Christ himself is the very embodiment of the divine-human dialogue: in him, Head of the human race, all humanity communes with the Trinity. By our extraordinary union with the Word of God through the humanity of Christ in his Mystical Body, and under the encompassing guidance of the omniscient Spirit, who dwells in the Church (1 Cor. 3:16–17) and in our hearts (Gal. 4:6), the word of Christ—the perfection of the divine-human exchange—dwells in us abundantly. We are enabled to hear the Word of God

(1 Cor. 2:12) and to speak it (1 Pt. 1:12). Not only do we participate in Christ's mission; we are incorporated actively into his contemplation. For Our Lord in his Mystical Body is the focus of all prayer and apostolate: in him, through his Sacrament the Church, both currents of supernatural life compenetrate, the one complementing the other, both together manifesting the inexhaustible riches, immanent and externalized, of the Incarnation.

By its very nature, therefore, our prayer is ecclesial. Even when uttered in solitude (in imitation, terrible and blessed, of the divine solitariness), it is communitarian. It is never the classical Greek notion of contemplation, *monos pros monon*, alone before the Alone: it is always bound up with the entire People of God, and rooted, in the concreteness of time and space, to the specific position (of pastor or militant or parent) that we hold in the Church. For in God's designs the perspective of the whole Church dominates our contemplation as well as our apostolate and, in doing so, sustains and develops them in their individuality. As with our apostolic activities, divine grace is distributed to our prayer essentially towards the building up of the Mystical Body of Christ (Eph. 4:7–12). Consequently authentic prayer is not an escape, an abstraction from the apostolate that we engage in according to our position in the Church; it is qualified by the actual function of our ecclesiastical role. Not only does it pervade our day's activities, it is adapted to their rhythm: only thus can it orient it towards God.

All genuine prayer is a prayer of the Church, gathered up in the vast stream of worship that rises, in daring, triumphant trust, to the divinity through Christ. But its central current is the Church's liturgy, with its movement concentrated in the focus of the eucharistic prayer-action. This liturgical prayer should be the norm of our personal attempts, their nourishment and even their pre-eminent expression.

For, in the first place, it is only God who can speak fittingly to God. The Church, Christ's Bride in whom the Spirit dwells in fullness, knows how to speak God's human language—in fact, repeatedly speaks his very own words. The Church has no use for the impotency of mystical babblings nor for incipient, "swollen words" (Mt. 6:7): her special concern is the sincere utterance that is vitalized by the simple immediacy and fecundity of God's revealed word. It is, therefore, from the Church (particularly in the sacrament of Christ's Sacrifice wherein we receive the Word as word and the Word as flesh) that we learn how to pray as God wills, and release ourselves, in disciplined liberty, from the bondage of human caprice.

And, secondly, the structural dynamic of the Church's liturgy is adapted to the inner rhythm of our existence, *and thereby to our apostolic endeavors.* Unfortunately, we moderns, "angry and uprooted," living in a civilization that is, in great part, dislocated from the measured pulse of the whole universe, fail to recognize the profound significance of the Christian liturgical cycle: how, in its measured consonance with man's beginning, growth and fulfillment, and with his dependence on the seasons and on the very motion of the heavens, it can best help us integrate our prayer and apostolate.

The fundamental rhythm of all created being consists in a balanced alternation of expansion-contraction, of building-up and breaking-down. In nature, for instance, there is the succession of day and night, and in man, who is providentially related to the total complex of nature, there is the corresponding quest and relaxation. The Christian liturgy, with its heritage in the synagogal tradition, is attuned to this basic rhythm that governs our life. With morning it would have us awaken to God's speech to us in the wonders of his creation, and to the conscious resumption of our role in Christ's redemptive mission. Its prayer, Lauds, is essentially a disinterested upsurge of divine praise, and a response to God's summons that re-echoes the exultant cry of the Word-made-Flesh to his Heavenly Father (Heb. 10:7). From meditation on Scripture it brings us to active participation in the eucharistic sacrifice, the supreme expression of our prayer and action in and by and with Our Lord, the mystic height of our daily existence towards which all advances and all returns.

Now unfolds the program of our day's work. Intermittently throughout our activities, and in the midst of our apostolate with its constant hazard of absorption in vain activism, Mother Church (graphically evidenced in the Benedictine Rule) would have us intersperse our efforts with meetings with God, in the midst of morning preoccupations, at the noonday pause, and as evening approaches. These deliberate turnings to God during which we ask his blessings on ourselves and our activities are not intended to distract from our obligations, but rather are designed to permeate and fill them with the climate of God's presence, and to glorify him in the more perfect execution of our duties: prayer may never be an escapism!

At sunset the Liturgy, in Vespers, would have us recapitulate our day's happenings, with their achievements and vicissitudes and failures—their pattern an echo of the experiences of the People of God in the Old Testament—and leads us to contemplate God's redemptive intervention in human history. Its rhythm then advances to the praise of God in himself, thus enclosing, with Lauds, our whole day in two movements of divine glorification.

But night, with its universal return to the sources of life, must not be a mere vacuum in our existence; it, too, must be directed to God. For our very relaxation and remaking in sleep can be transformed, by our deliberate orientation to God, into an uninterrupted hymn of praise: "My soul desires thee in the night, and in my spirit seeks thee." (Ps. 26:7). The apostle is aware of the mysterious, providential affinity between night and contemplation (Ps. 118:55, 62; Mt. 25:6; Eph. 5:14), and recalls how Christ himself, our Exemplar, was accustomed (Lk. 22:39; 6:12) to pray within its quiet obscurity.

Our efforts, therefore, should aim at comforming our schedule of prayer to the objectives and rhythm of the Liturgy if we wish it not only to be imbued with the spirit of the Church, and therefore of Christ, but to remain practical, realistic. Thus our prayer will be rooted in the concrete details of charity, and not wallow in abstractions; and our apostolate will be safeguarded from the pretensions of natural activism. As Karl Rahner, S.J., puts it, like Mary, Queen of Apostles, we will be active in our contemplation and contemplative in our action.

21 * The Word of God

And as the rain and the snow come down from heaven, and return no more thither, but soak the earth, and water it, and make it to spring, and give seed to the sower, and bread to the eater, so shall my word be, which shall go forth from my mouth: it shall not return to me void, but it shall do whatever I please, and shall prosper in the things for which I sent it.

(Is. 55:10–11)

The (revealed) truth in human words is not meant merely to go on being monotonously repeated in stereotyped phrases in theology textbooks. It is meant to come into living contact with the individual Christian, to take on flesh and blood, penetrate his heart and mind and bring him the truth. Each man anew has to make it his own. Each man, with his own experiences, his own vocation and his whole spiritual situation, which is not only that of Catholic Christianity, but the general spiritual situation of his time, must individually hear God's message anew. And because a man's faith is not the message that could be heard but the message he does hear, and because the truth of revelation cannot exist on earth in one eternally static and valid form, but only as it is actually believed by men, the plain unchanging truth of the Gospel, as it is actually heard and understood by men of every age, must bear the mark of that age upon it. If it doesn't, or doesn't sufficiently, this does not make it timeless and universally valid: it is much more likely to mean that it wears the garb of another age, which men have become used to, and because it is ancient and customary, have falsely come to think of it as the expression of the eternally unchanging truth of the Gospel. The freezing of the form in which the truth of the Gospel is expressed is in fact a dangerous symptom of indifference. . . .

Carl Rahner

Christ preaches through Christ.

St. Augustine

G. K. CHESTERTON once remarked that, in his opinion—one that was invariably worthwhile—our twentieth century suffers, not so much from a moral collapse, as from a mental breakdown. The validity of his observation can be seen from the modern dethronement of truth, an ominous symptom of today's dehumanization of man.

Until recently even errors were advanced in the name of truth. The presumptuous theologies of heretics and even the absurd philosophies of nihilists all appealed to the norm of truth. But, in our time, we have heard Nazism claim Race and Communism declare Class as the ultimate norm for the acceptance of any statement or thesis. An abhorrent relativism continues to infiltrate into everyday life. Its evil is now hardly questioned! A contingent standard of expediency has replaced truth, the validity of an opinion no longer depending on its conformity to reality but its usefulness, for example. The very notion of objective truth is tacitly ignored.

This gradual perversion of the human mind is further evidenced in the progressive corruption of language, the vehicle of truth. The Word of God perfectly reflects God; in a finite manner man's word reflects him. But today we witness a tragic anarchy in human language. So very often words are lacking in shape and decision: sentences are but debris of words, their contents scattered in all directions, each individual part torn from context. Language so dismembered is no longer able to provide articulation, to communicate truth; in fact, there is little communication, only dialogue. This chaos in language reflects the fragmentation within modern man himself.

Confronted by the contemporary dethronement of truth, the Catholic is conscious of his duty to defend and serve truth. With a liberating alertness of mind, avoiding gullibility as well as smugness and pedantry, he is humble and reverent before objective reality. He develops that resonance of mind whereby he perceives that truth is not something opaque, a mere surface, but of profound richness and depth; and so his consistent, exuberant reaction to reality is always the "wondering" which, according to Plato, is the beginning of knowledge. Moreover, his language is not a thing misshapen and eviscerated; it is a vital communication.

But much still remains to be attempted if mankind is to be

freed from the morass of error in which it flounders. For the exigencies of man's nature, called to a supernatural destiny, demand more than contact with the strong reality of this cosmos. Man desperately needs insertion into the supernatural history of salvation, the Paschal Mystery that penetrates and yet transcends the human condition in its total demensions.

The one who is truly Christian, and not merely marginal, is aware that he must cooperate in the realization of this prodigious task by bringing God's Word to his fellow men—the Word that is actually God's efficacious invitation to enter into the history of salvation.

From the distant beginnings of mankind's adventure, God has progressively revealed himself, particularly to the saint and to the poet. In the manner of a tremendous lover he has manifested himself in the signs that burst from the sacramental reality of the universe of things—a mysterious unveiling that opens to possibilities of awesome proportions in the scientific discoveries and technological achievements of our time. Even more profound has been the divine revelation within the context of human existence: the immense human, historical duration presents a wealth of perspectives that reveal divine depths and plumb ever deeper into the infinite abyss of the divine fullness.

But, in unique manner, God took hold of the people of Israel; and through the unfolding of their living situation—a concentration, in shattering poignancy, of the universal human experience in its various dimensions—he revealed himself in the special mode of human expression that we call language. The Word of God thus made use of the word of man, and continues to do so: "It is I, Yahweh, who speak with precision, and I express myself in true words" (Is. 45:19).

True words (substantial, potent, not garrulous babblings)

are an integral part of man's personality: emerging freely from the full silence within the core of his being, they manifest his most intimate nature. The total humanism of biblical man, representative of all mankind, thus became the very center of God's speech, expressing progressively not only the inner mystery of man himself, but also that of the Absolute.

Speech, however, is ordered to its perfection in life; it must transcend itself in action that engages the whole person; it is, in fact, the beginning of total self-commitment. In awesome, humble earnestness Almighty God has condescended to enter into this constitutive rhythm of human expression, moving the divine "inhumanization" (as Max Weber happily put it) to the unutterable mystery of the Incarnation. The Word of God was made flesh that could be seen and heard and touched. And so in Christ the merciful love of God achieved its consummate revelation—one that continues in and through his Mystical Body, the Church, in whose sacramental cosmos, and only there, revealed truth is made living and effective (Heb. 4:12).

The structural dynamism of this revelation is essentially one of dialogue, a vital communication, a personal I-Thou relationship, between God and man, and it is an exchange that is realized between the Almighty and man-as-member-of-his-Church.

Israel, the first phase of this Church, was organized into an organic unity by the personal intervention of Yahweh: "And I said to thee . . . Live . . ." (Ez. 16:3–13). As related in the Book of Exodus (cc. 3, 19, 20, 24) Moses, commanded by Yahweh, convoked the first real assembly (Hebrew, *Quahal*) of the scattered clans. He proposed to them God's offer: "I will make you a kingdom of priests, and a consecrated nation . . . if you obey me and respect my Convenant" (Ex.

19:5–6). Believing in the divine promises, the Israelites formally pledged obedience to the Law, and offered a sacrifice that symbolically united Yahweh and his people by sprinkling of blood. The covenant was then completed by Yahweh's acceptance of the sacrifice. Henceforth, throughout their tortuous history, this people would remain conscious of themselves as God's Chosen; though often refractory to divine grace, they would reconfirm this holy alliance (2 Kings 23; Neh. 8:10), always within the same structural dynamism of the first: proclamation of God's Word, man's reply and the sealing of the Covenant by sacrifice.

It is in the Christ, the human incarnation of God's redeeming love, that this exchange between the Divinity and Man is finally realized: he is the very embodiment of the Covenant, transformed, interiorized, elevated. "In the same Person," observes Father E. Schillebeeckx, O.P., "there was achieved the perfection both of the divine invitation and of the human response." *Christ Jesus is the consummate Dialogue between God and Man; he is the New Covenant.* Obedient even unto death and now gloriously risen, he in whom all history converges and takes on meaning, draws to himself by a mysterious gravitation all mankind, all being, to participate in this alliance. And he does so through his Church, his permanent incarnation in time and space. So the Church is the continued realization of the Covenant. Within its organic, mysterious reality the prophetic proclamation of the Word of God (particularly within the assembly of the Mass—the convocation through which Christ actually sustains his Church), man's response (in and by and with Christ), and the sacrificial ratification (in the Sacrament of Christ's sacrifice) are extended throughout mankind's exodus to its holy destiny in the messianic future.

Now, the Word of God, proclaimed from within the Church by the Apostles' successors and their collaborators, is actualized by the sacraments—in consummate manner by the Eucharist. "What is said exists, what is proclaimed is done" (Father A. M. Roquet, O.P.). Word moves to action, expands to the supreme action of sacrifice; it becomes living, efficacious, saving, sanctifying. "What you have just heard is today accomplished!" (Lk. 16:14–20).

The Word of God, therefore, an announcement of God's coming in Christ, and of his salvific will, is an invitation to all men to enter into the Covenant; and within the sacramental structure of the Church, and there only, it is no dead letter, no mere external message (2 Cor. 3:3; Heb. 4:12; Heb. 8:8–12), but a force that creates from within the "heart that knows how to listen" (1 Kings 3:9, a personal actualization in the history of salvation.

These considerations, though all too brief, indicate the apostolic disposition that must be ours towards God's Word.

Fundamental is the receptivity, active and thoroughly sacramental, that presupposes a sincere enthusiastic effort to appreciate the material as well as the spiritual significance of symbol; the "true word," spacious, powerful, volatile, transcending itself in action; the "sacrament" of the universe and the "sacrament" of human history—an orientation that rises from the broad calm of inner silence.

It is the conviction, illuminated by faith, that God's authentic Word is possible only from within his Church. Only God can speak fittingly about God, observed Pascal; and only in his Church is the revealed Word animated by the Spirit who inspired it, thereby rendering it personal, communicative, assimilable. Moreover, God's Word becomes *event*, germinative, operative, only within his Church, the Sacrament that renders present what it proclaims: no longer is it a mere witness to the past, it is a living experience.

It is the zeal, propelled forward by love of God, to bring to all men his invitation that they enter into the history of salvation, the transfigured world created by the sacraments; ultimately to invite them to participate in the mystery of the Eucharist in which that history is most fully realized.

It is both contemplation and apostolate, the one overflowing and being fulfilled in the other.

Within the communal compass of the Church, where liturgical word is accomplished in sacramental action, biblical word is no piece of arid ratiocination or sentimental fantasy, the unbearably anachronistic dreaming that evokes the scorn of a modern Celsus. Ultimately this revealed Word is no mere idea, it is a Person: its contemplation is not just the acquisition of speculative knowledge, but a personal, prayerful encounter.

And it is a recognition that inevitably results in the engagement of apostolate. By his witnessing in charity the apostle is not like Beckett's character in *The Unnameable*, "in words. made of words" only; no "forgetful hearer, but a true doer" (Ja. 1:15). Through zealous acceptance of the sacramental word the apostle participates in God's present intervention in human history, that is, in the unfolding here and now of Christ's Paschal Mystery. Through his apostolate the word that became event in the sacrament is prolonged concretely in the diversified context of human experience.

He thus becomes Christ's letter (2 Cor. 3:3), written by the Holy Spirit on his most intimate being, inviting all men to enter into the history of salvation, a letter that by the grace of the same Spirit attracts and vitalizes.

In sum, the true Christian adventurously pursues truth in its length and breadth, in its heighth and depth, because he realizes that in doing so he approaches Christ; or rather, that he grows in the very likeness of Christ. Thus transformed in truth, his mission is a participation in that of the Word made flesh: to bring to our world, swallowed in the monstrous vortex of error, the truth that alone brings freedom (Jn. 8:32).

22 * Poverty

The foxes have dens, and the birds of the air have nests, but the Son of Man has nowhere to lay his head.

(Mt. 8:20)

For you know the graciousness of our Lord Jesus Christ—how, being rich, He became poor for our sake, that by His poverty, you might become rich.

(2 Cor. 8:9)

Evangelical poverty is a warning of man's insufficiency and his consequent need for God. It is a denial of the primacy of the economic and of the capacity of temporal goods to satisfy the heart of man. It is a renunciation of the search to fulfill our destiny in this world, or to find safegards against what are deep and fatal evils, such as sin and death. It is the wisdom which disillusions us about the fever for gold and power, and teaches us that goodness, love, charity, peace and greatness of soul are not acquired by means of money and wealth. It is dignified and industrious patience in the face of living with a scarcity of economic resources and in the midst of modest social conditions. It is conducive to praying, to working well, to hoping, to giving and loving, because it teaches confidence in Providence and a recognition of the worth of things and moral good. It is liberation of the spirit which, freed from the distractions of inferior goods, can act and love as spirit.

Pope Paul VI

THE MODERN WORLD abhors physical poverty as an unsightly disgrace, a downgrade in its straining after "progress," a nausea in contemporary life. It is something that must be attacked methodically and unremittingly by social engineering.

Consequently, in the secularist evaluation, the poor are no longer regarded as the "privileged objects of the Savior's providence," persons demanding, by reason of God's sacred image in them—no matter how distorted it be at times—a reflection of the attitude that Christ had for all of us, rich and poor alike. Instead, the poor are organized, inquisitioned, classified, and not infrequently humiliated and discredited. They are even seduced by the new "hygiene" to forfeit their unborn, in return for which they are offered a sterile loneliness.

If the modern world looks upon physical poverty as an affront, it deems as madness the Christian spirit of poverty. It may concede to its simplicity a certain charm, even grandeur, but will denounce it as absurdly ineffective so far as civilization's onward march is concerned. Sometimes it may consider it of some therapeutic or artistic value, but soon dismisses it as a futile, anachronistic groping after illusions, something primitively noble that may be admired in the romantic figure of Francis of Assisi, but definitely not to be lived by us moderns.

The sad fact is that, in practice, not a few of us agree with the world. We are so empty of God that we frantically attempt to fill up the void within our being with matter that can be seen, measured, compared. With a zeal that ever grows more feverish, we seek to possess things—and be possessed by them.

Subsisting in this material, unauthentic existence, we give ourselves in scattered "apostolate" to others; but, as de Lubac warns, "what interests us in others is not their true being, 'the image of God to be restored', but that they provide us merely with an opportunity of satisfying our need of exteriorization. . . ." In our anxiety to promote, "extend," ourselves we tend to monopolize persons rather than lead them to Christ. We would even absorb them spiritually, reducing them to objects, while cunningly concealing our avarice under the guise of apostolic enthusiasm. No longer do we know them in themselves, but rather within the limited confines of our Ego, we measure them according to our needs: we cannot truly communicate with them. The entire supernatural work of the Church we now judge by the world's implacable standard, tangible Success. We would even presume to build Christ's Mystical Body on salesmanship and cement.

By contrast, Christian poverty is of the realm of reality. It is the total detachment from all interior and external possessions—the entire span from spiritual comfort and one's reputation to physical well-being and conveniences. It is the chalice of one's existence scoured clean, and open with the active receptivity of love, to God's presence and action. It is absolute disinheritance (2 Cor. 6:10), the utter abandonment of personal acquisitiveness—and all this as an expression, in purest simplicity, in complete freedom, of love for God. As Jean Daniélou puts it, "Poverty may be called the epiphany of love," for more than anything else, it manifests our love for God: in it there is nothing left but love, as it was in Bethlehem's poverty that "Christ's love was most simply shown."

Therefore, the Christian predilection for actual and spiritual poverty must not be confused with the pretensions of Ebionism, the exaggeration of poverty that eventually leads to the complete damning of God's creation and of human achievements. The instinct to possess is implanted in man's nature; as creature he needs to be augmented and completed by other than himself, ultimately by the One who alone is self-sufficient. The Christian emphasis is not a condemnation but an absolute rule of spiritual perfection: that "nothing should be possessed as if it were not possessed, used as if it were not used" (M. Michel Labourette, O.P.). Poverty, then, is not an absolute, but a positive means at the service of charity. Life according to the "Gospel's form," to quote St. Francis of Assisi, must accordingly be guided by the exigencies of charity, for example, the obligations of one's state of life: what matters is that we possess and use the holy detachment.

On the other hand, Christian poverty must not be identified with an anaemic so-called "spiritualized" poverty, a dissimulation that has nothing poor about it. Such gross hypocrisy is an outrage in a world where countless humans still bow low in destitution, engrossed in the devouring pursuit of the bare necessities of life. True Christian poverty is a living, practised affirmation of abandonment to Divine Providence, one that is incarnated in the fabric of tangible, everyday life. It is a real liberation, an honest, courageous freedom that opens magnanimously to the plenitude of God and of all His creation. Perhaps never before has there been such a desperate need for the prophetic witnessing to these ideals.

Paradoxically (always the startling, Christian paradox!), in the tradition of the Old and New Testaments, this total abandonment, with all its deep searing trials, is incomparable riches. "Mine are the heavens and mine is the earth. Mine are

all men: the just are mine and the sinners. And the angels are
mine, and the Mother of God, and all things are mine. And
God himself is mine and for me! Hear then, my soul! What
do you seek and ask for? All this is mine and all is for thee"
(St. John of the Cross). It is the very possession of God, in his
being and activity, and of all creation in God. It is the depri-
vation, in imitation of the Poor Man, whereby we, though
beggars, find all things in our belonging, *and bring riches to
many* (2 Cor. 6:8–10). For Christian poverty invites the fullness of God: in its climate the Holy Spirit accomplishes the
great designs of apostolate—such that only those whose being
and effort are actuated by its spirit are true apostles: theirs is
the kingdom of heaven (Mt. 5:3).

It is the empty net that God, in his infinite wisdom, continues to fill with a miraculous catch.

23 * Self-Immolation

> *And James and John, the sons of Zebedee, came to
> him, saying "Master, we want thee to do for us
> whatever we ask." But he said to them, "What do
> you want me to do for you?" And they said, "Grant
> us that we may sit, one at thy right hand, and the
> other at thy left hand, in Thy glory." But Jesus said
> to them, "You do not know what you are asking for.
> Can you drink of the cup of which I drink, or be
> baptized with the baptism with which I am to be
> baptized?" And they said to him, "We can." And
> Jesus said to them, "Of the cup that I drink, you
> shall drink; and with the baptism with which I am
> baptized, you shall be baptized; but as for sitting*

*at my right hand or at my left, that is not mine to
give, but it belongs to those for whom it has been
prepared."*

(Mk. 10:35–40)

*It seems to me that Jesus Christ allowed only his
wounds to be touched after his Resurrection.*

Pascal

*If you were to bring together saints fit for canoni-
zation to collaborate in the same work, they would
probably be a cause of suffering to each other.*

Abbot Marmion, O.S.B.

To be true apostles it behooves us to be *men crucified—*
crucified in Christ the Savior. Otherwise we are impostors.
We claim that we witness to Christ crucified (1 Cor. 1:23),
aspiring to help draw all mankind to the God-Man lifted high
on the infamous gibbet (Jn. 12:22); but we refuse to manifest
in our own selves the mortification of Jesus (2 Cor. 4:10). In
effect, the Cross has become for us a disconcerting foolishness
and weakness; we turn from its repugnance and rely on the
wisdom of the wise. And our apostolate becomes a sterile, deceptive thing.

Sören Kierkegaard, that lonely pilgrim of the Absolute who
tried to alert the "Christian" world to its dire bankruptcy,
often insisted, with profound spiritual intuition, that suffering
is the element "in which that which is religious begins to
breathe." Is not the "lull and deadness" of our apostolic
efforts due to the fact that we are not sufficiently acquainted
with the overpowering reality of the Cross?

St. Paul bluntly assures us that Christ crucified is the Wisdom of God (1 Cor. 1:25). No matter where we turn in the

Christian life, we revert to the divine poignancy of God's redemptive love, to the "sacredly terrifying mystery" of the Cross—the indispensable, complementary rhythm in the Paschal mystery that effects our resurrection in the glorified humanity of Christ. This law of Christianity, the paradox of life in death, governs the development of all Christian contemplative and apostolic life. We may attempt to deny it, by a desiccating escapism, by a resentful abdication, by a struggle entrenched in pride, even by a morbid egocentricity, a kind of dolorism that makes us recoil within ourselves from divine grace; but the great opportunity of the Cross remains. It must, for we need the Cross.

To reach the Promised Land we must pass through the fatigue and aridity of the desert. To be transformed in the pure light of his holiness we must first experience the night of Christ's agony. This is the essential Paschal rhythm of the Christian apostolic as well as contemplative life, a truth that cannot be repeated too often.

In the first place, the action of our apostolate demands constant purification. For the leaven of self-love pervades deep into all that we do, pressing us forward to the vain pursuit of vain success—to the extent that we would do violence even to the slow action of grace and to the inviolable liberty of human persons. Our egotistical viewpoints and personal ambitions, all that contravenes God's plan, must be purified in the crucible of the Cross: this is an absolute necessity. But more: even all that is genuinely apostolic in our activity must be purified; *it must surpass all that appears to be our limit.* "Every branch that bears fruit, the Father will cleanse that it may bear more fruit" (Jn. 15:2, 3). The cutting is ruthless, but it is done in order that we exceed ourselves. The law of the Cross is not inhuman, but superhuman, a truth especially manifest in the towering lives of Mary and of Abraham.

Secondly, we must become identified with Christ crucified. The process of purification that we have mentioned—the emptying of all that is impure—cannot be accomplished unless there be a corresponding "increase" of Christ within our being. In Baptism we have already been immersed in his death (Rom. 6:3–4); now throughout our lives, we must cooperate with the Holy Spirit in the progressive conforming of our entire persons to the passion of Our Lord (Phil. 3:10).

The trials of our apostolate offer abundant opportunities towards this configuration. St. Andrew of Crete penetratingly observed that "if there had been no Cross; it was waiting for him." And so with respect to ourselves: inherent in our apostolate are the pains of many harassments, fatigue, discouragements and disappointments that contribute to the making of our personal crosses.

In these we must confront the "scandal" of Christ, in the bitter doubts that will sometimes assail us regarding the very validity of our apostolate. How paltry and useless it can appear! We must learn through imperturbable confidence the profound significance of Christ's gentle warning to the Precursor: "Blessed is he that is not scandalized in me" (Mt. 11:6). And we must experience the burden of the messianic psalm that the dying Savior recalled in his atrocious torment: "My God, My God, why hast thou forsaken me?" (Ps. 21:1)

Thirdly, as apostles our vocation is to be saviors with Jesus, "the God who saves." As co-sufferers (2 Tm. 2:11–12), we too must be nailed to the universal cross (Gal. 2:10–20). Our mysterious destiny is to be "his surplus humanity" (Sister Elizabeth of the Trinity), his complement in suffering (Col. 1:24), through whom he continues to renew and apply the mystery of his redemptive Passion. We are to bear others in Christ (Phil. 1:10); and to do so we must undergo the pangs of this inscrutable, spiritual childbirth. Like St. Ignatius the Martyr, we have the privilege to be "God's wheat," willing to be broken on behalf of the multitude of persons who await his divinizing grace. Thus, truly identified with our bruised Savior, the drawing power of his virtue will continue in and through our lives, communicating to others the beginnings of our universal resurrection through his glorified humanity.

Can we share with Christ his chalice of suffering? Are we capable of weathering the apprenticeship of the Cross? Can we become co-victims with Christ?

Yes, but only provided we remain united with our divine Lord; provided we confidently turn to him for strength, and return again and again to the comtemplation of *his* Cross—the excruciating agony that he underwent for each one of us individually as well as for mankind as a whole (1 Jn. 2:2), and that he embraced in all its concrete, crushing physical-spiritual reality. Only thus can we come, not only to endure our personal crosses, but to love them.

Sad experience proves that otherwise we become insufferable in our sufferings. The mathematical repetition, and apparent insignificance of the usual, everyday harassments disgust and bore us. We become embittered by an unhealthy obsession of suffering in itself—of pain divorced from Christ and untransmuted by sacrificial love: the mystery of suffering can even become for us a damning, cruel absurdity.

It is only when we contemplate Christ crucified—and triumphant in his very crucifixion; when we realize that his Calvary is actually linked with every pain-filled moment of our own lives and those of our contemporaries, offering supernatural strength and peace to all of us in these moments. When we grow in the zealous awareness of our vocation as co-saviors with Christ, only then do our crosses become redemptively fertile, not only in time, but in eternity.

24 ✳ Sacrament of Christ's Sacrifice

And when the hour had come, he reclined at table, and the twelve apostles with him. "I have greatly desired to eat this passover with you before I suffer; for I say to you that I will eat of it no more, until it has been fulfilled in the Kingdom of God." And having taken a cup, he gave thanks and said, "Take this and share it among you; for I say to you I will not drink of the fruit of the vine, until the Kingdom of God comes." And having taken bread, he gave thanks and broke, and gave it to them saying, "This is my Body, which is being given for you; do this in remembrance of me." In like manner he took also the cup after the supper, saying, "This cup is the new covenant in my blood, which shall be shed for you."

(Lk. 22:14–20)

For as often as you shall eat this bread and drink this cup, you proclaim the death of the Lord, until he comes.

(1 Cor. 11:26)

If you are the Body of Christ, if you are his members, it is your own mystery which is placed upon the altar of the Lord; it is your own mystery which you receive.

St. Augustine

WE HAVE STRESSED the fact that to be apostles of Christ we must bear witness to him crucified: the only alternative is masquerade, a lie. Now, St. Paul reminds us that "as often as you shall eat this bread and drink this cup you proclaim the death of the Lord, until he comes" (1 Cor. 11:26). In other words, it is through vital participation in the Church's Eucharistic Action that we are capable of truly witnessing to our Redeemer—witnessing not merely as signs pointing beyond ourselves, but rather by way of an interpersonal relationship with Christ that, in turn, necessarily influences other persons.

Here we arrive at a consideration of the Eucharist, the measured ceremonial of gesture, act, word—the *liturgy*—that constitutes the supreme test of faith. In it God has sealed the New Covenant with the blood of his Son; in its ceremonial rite the God-Man has gathered up and placed the abundance of his redemptive destiny. This is the action that must vitalize all our apostolic activity.

For by definition apostolate is redemptive. And it can be such only by union with our Redeemer. Jesus Christ alone is the Just One and the Holy One (Acts 3:14) and he alone is our Justice, our Sanctification, and our Redemption (1 Cor. 1:30). Only by living contact with the Eternal Priest can our efforts share in the tremendous power of his sacrifice.

But how achieve this union? The transfigured Christ has withdrawn from our tangible world of empirical experience. True. Christ is now in glory. But we must remember that he "appears in God's sight on our behalf" (Heb. 9:24), arrayed in the fullness of his sacrificial role, as priest and victim; and that, in this sacrificial state Christ, until the end of time, will continue to "claim from his Father his promise to bestow the Holy Spirit" (Acts 2:33). The Father has *already* poured out this Spirit in the Church, Christ's Mystical Body—a fact we can experience for ourselves in the "new wonders" (Is. 43:18), the sacraments, of which the Eucharist is the sum and center. Precisely in these sacraments (particularly let it be repeated, in the Eucharist) do we encounter in a quasi-bodily mode our glorified Lord, and personally, dynamically commune with him. Of course, communion with Christ, and through Christ with the entire Trinity, is attainable in prayer and mystical union; but, as Father E. Schillebeeckx, O.P., points out, "because of the spiritual-tangible dimension of our human make-up, it is through the sacraments, approached in faith, that our existential interrelationship with the Kyrios is more fully realized and developed by the Holy Spirit."

The Eucharist is the memorial of Christ's redemptive historical existence, specifically of his death on the Cross, awesome action in which he was both priest and victim. It is the incomparable, the *anamnesis*, *Sacrament* of Christ's sacrifice: that is, it signifies and *contains* the entire reality of the sacrifice of the Cross. "The instant Christ's representative speaks his words over the bread and wine," writes Guardini, "Christ steps from eternity into place and hour, to become vitally present with the fullness of his redemptory power in the form of the particular created species of bread and wine." Thus, in the Eucharistic Action the active presence of Jesus Christ, in his sacrificial state, is inserted into our human time; his sacrifice is reproduced sacramentally, and its efficacy is put at our disposal, individually and collectively, in our immediate situation.

Christ's sacrifice as a historical event, situated in and dominated by particular time and space, is a reality that is irrevocably past. However, it was a human act personalized by the Son of God, incarnating in divinely poignant splendor his interior act of sacrifice for mankind. Being a personal action of God, it is imperishable, eternally present. The second Divine Person of the Trinity continues in his interior act of sacrifice. But now the human mode of expression of this sacrifice is different. Its eternal contemporaneity is now humanly incarnate in a new, mysterious heavenly manner, utterly beyond our comprehension—and beyond immediate, tangible contact by us who still live in untransfigured earthly condition. Only through the sacraments, above all in the Eucharist, can we make quasi-bodily contact with the eternally-present redemptive act of sacrifice of the God-Man.

A truth of capital importance to note is that the eternally-present interior act of redemption of the Son of God always refers to the bloody sacrifice of Christ consummated in time. While it is from the glorified *Kyrios* that the Eucharistic action (and the other sacraments) receive their efficacy, it is by Christ's Cross that such communication of supernatural power was originally achieved.

In its total character as sacrifice the Mass, supreme action of the Mystical Body of Christ, moves to its consummation in communion. As we have seen, Christ enters into our time and space as Victim in the plenitude of his redemptory power, under signs that betoken the shedding of blood. But he remains present under the forms of bread and wine precisely in order that, through our reception of the consecrated offerings, he may exercise his deifying action on us and on his entire Church.

Thus, the Eucharistic mystery is the Church's sacrificial banquet of the new, eternal Covenant. For it is the body of Christ, the very substance of God. In the order of divine life it is truly the Christian's food whereby the vital reality of which his soul was made since Baptism receives strength and growth.

But it must be added that the Christian receives the Eucharist not alone, but as one with the Christian community, and with Christ himself as companion who, according to his human nature, also feeds on the divine substance (Ap. 3:20). *The Eucharist is, therefore, a meal shared:* "The meal of friendship and unity with our victorious Lord."

However, this concept is still inadequate. We must attempt to envisage the Eucharist in all its amplitude. Guardini pertinently comments that the reality of the Eucharist as "meal" must be balanced by its reality as "encounter," otherwise there is the danger of reducing the sacrament to a mere object, a thing handled. The whole truth is that the "true bread," the "food and drink," the "flesh for the life of the world" is the glorified God-Man "who comes down from heaven" (Jn. 6:33, 57). The Eucharistic mystery is, therefore, a meeting of persons, a reciprocal communion: through the instrumentality of the sacramental species the Christian enters into a vital, interpersonal relationship with the Lord.

The consequences of this encounter are momentous. In the first place there is a deepening of the Christian's incorporation into Christ. The strength of Christ penetrates into the depths of his being, into the very union of his soul and body, even to the extent of perfecting his body's right to resurrection and curbing the sway of the flesh over the spirit. His entire existence grows in the likeness of Christ, he becomes more identified with his Lord; for through the Eucharist Christ gradually transforms the Christian into himself, communicating to him his very soul, his virtues, his dispositions—above all his love. The pre-eminent effect of this Sacrament is, actually, the communication of the act of supernatural love, which, though a grace that passes and must be renewed, leaves the Christian in a state of greater love for God through Christ, a love that inevitably proves itself in dedicated apostolate.

But not only does the Eucharist effect an increase of the Christian's incorporation in Christ; there is also—to quote de Lubac—a *"con-corporation of the whole Church in one mysterious unity."*

"The one bread makes us one body; though we are many in number, the same bread is shared by all" (1 Cor. 10:7). United in Christian charity in our reception of the Eucharist —in our sacramental encounter with the Lord—this unique food gathers us all into a mysterious unity in itself. St. Cyril of

Alexandria expressed the cherished teaching of the Fathers of the Church when he observed that "through one only body, his own, he sanctifies his faithful in mystic communion, making them one body with him and among themselves," such that the Eucharist is, indeed, the symbol of the Church (Council of Trent): the real body of Christ is both the cause and the sign of his Mystical Body: more expressly, it is the sign that effects what it signifies. Under the impulse of the Holy Spirit this divine food builds up the Church through the individual Christian, advancing it towards its full stature, a pledge, therefore, of mankind's fully revealed encounter with Christ in his Second Coming, and through Christ, with the Trinity in beatific possession.

From the above, though merely an outline, it should be evident that the Eucharist, the sacrament that "contains the whole mystery of our salvation," is the heart of the apostolate; for the very rhythm of the Eucharistic operation is reflected in the movement of the apostolate. Apostolic activity is nothing other than the burgeoning, the effulgence of the Eucharistic action from within the interior life of the Christian community, from within its depths. The "fervor of love," the proper effect of Eucharistic communion, as we mentioned above— necessarily radiates in fecund love of one's neighbor in Christ, and in zealous participation in the Church's apostolate; for love demands that more and more children of man be brought to the God who is love.

Without the Eucharist there is no life (Jn. 6:54), there is no fruitful activity, there is no apostolate. Instead, like the barren fig tree, our attempts, claiming to be what they are not, are already cursed with an avalanche of poisonous failure and crushing disappointment, spiritual penury.

But through the Eucharist there is nourishment, growth,

vital apostolate; *there is the Church, Christ's Mystical Body,* voicing humanity's great thanksgiving to the Triune God.

25 * Apostolic Joy

Show them that they have no other duty in the world than joy!

Paul Claudel

If I am to believe in their Savior, they must sing better songs; his disciples must appear more like persons saved!

Nietzsche

SOMETIMES it seems that our twentieth century, with its climate drenched in unwholesome skepticism, opens its horizons onto hell itself. Dread, despair, anguish: they form the motif that interpenetrates modern man's thinking, a theme preoccupied with the negative aspects of his existence. For humanity today experiences, with deep poignancy, the failure of the deceptive dreams cherished by the Enlightenment. With the unprecedented chaos and cruelty unleashed during the past half decade, the utopian belief in incessant progress and the idolatrous trust in science as the universal panacea have met with cruel disappointment. The human person finds himself swept up in an accelerated, historical process that emphasizes his vulnerability and loneliness; within the increasing complexity of society's structure, social engineering reduces him more and more to a mere element within the crowd—and the crowd, in turn, is manipulated by the new, powerful mass media. Thus, living in an "age of troubles," and straining towards a future hidden in precariousness, modern man feels himself engulfed in a black tide of gloom. Certainly there are the outstanding growth in technology, the building of the great cities, the new dimensions in pioneering; and there are the lights and the sounds and the pleasures. But the widespread anxiety cannot be denied; nor can the increasing disappearance of joy—the joy that Dostoevsky recognized "can never be godless."

In the midst of this floundering atmosphere of doubt and foreboding St. Paul's repeated cry of "Rejoice!", both greeting and commanding challenge, takes on a special urgency. For the reproaches of the secularist are too often valid: not a few of us Christian apostles, who are supposed to be joyful in full measure (Jn. 17:12) at all times (Phil. 4:4–6), succumb instead to the prevalent, devitalizing pessimism, and wear a spurious Catholicism that publicizes defeat instead of indicating renewal in our triumphant Savior. We who are entrusted with the continuation of Christ's mission—the "great, joyous work" mentioned by Newman—the implementation of the "good news of great rejoicing" (Lk. 2:10–11); are bogging down in morbid subjectivity and feeding on unhealthy melancholy, rather than meeting all vicissitudes with Christian serenity! (Col. 1:11). The spectacle is a sorry one.

We must never forget that Christ's mission began with an "emptying" (Phil. 2:7)—and that our sharing in his mission must begin in like manner. Total abnegation, motivated by love of God, is the necessary condition for fruitful apostolic life. Paradoxically (Mt. 10:30) it is by this death to self that we possess ourselves and are capable of giving our service to Christ in others. And it is by the ecstasy of this abnegation (using the word "ecstasy" in its etymological meaning: a going out of oneself) that we bring true joy to our modern world where it is so conspicuous by its absence.

For our love of God—more pure, more intense, and more expansive in proportion to our "emptying" of self—is already love enjoying, *amor fruens*. It is distinguishable from all other loves, which, when the persons or things that are loved are absent, result in sadness. Love of God is in itself both love and possession—the two prerequisites of joy. By the very fact of our loving God, he lives in us: "He who dwells in love, dwells in God and God in him" (1 Jn. 4:16). We are capable of "possessing" the divine Trinity of Persons who love one another infinitely, each himself only by relation to the others— the God who is unfathomable joy because he is love eternally shared!

Thus, living in the splendor of joy that emanates from the divinity, we, in turn, will radiate its tranquil, sustaining force throughout our milieux, gradually transfiguring the universe of persons and things, rendered opaque by sin, with an expanding incandescence.

For joy has qualities analogous to those of light. It gives of itself; and because of this mysterious abnegation, it illuminates. In spontaneously offering ourselves to God, in and by and with Christ, we share ourselves with all being, absorbing it in his blessing.

But this consuming action of joy demands that it be replenished constantly in the terrible and glorious purity of God. We must go again and again into the holy place where he dwells in inaccessible light (Ps. 42), to the one who is Light (1 Jn. 1:5). That is, we must go to the sacred altar—symbol of our encounter with the divine majesty, the table on which we offer sacrifice and through which we communicate with God —because the total offering of ourselves in sacrifice is absolutely necessary.

Only by offering our sacrifice to be united with and transformed by the sacrifice of Christ can we, the members of his

Mystical Body, participate in and irradiate his joy: for the eucharistic mystery is the sacramental sign of the ultimate, beatific possession of God in Christ Jesus, of eternal transfiguration in the blazing plenitude of the Trinity.

Thus, united with Christ in his eucharistic sacrifice, allowing him to communicate to us his dispositions, we will become more fully aware of the mysteries stirring beneath the turbulence of our twentieth century. Anchored in the strength and tranquility of his joy, we will be able to resist the evil fascination of the vortex that lures to an existence that is closed, shrunken, estranged, incoherent. We will look beyond the blood-stained mud and the destruction and the depravity to the liberation of all creation, and the consummation of mankind in the unity of Christ's perfection; and we will, right now in the palpable present, joyfully collaborate in the unfolding of this tremendous enterprise.

But let us be careful to remember that, by its very nature, there is nothing affected in the expression of Christian joy. In the apostolate it manifests itself in the unaffected graciousness of good humor (the gradual disappearance of which Chesterton, interestingly, associated with the denial of the eucharistic mystery). This is the unfailing, hearty disposition at once strong and limber, that attracts others to Christ and, at the same time, prevents us from falling into the self-absorption of despair or, as Grandmaison pointed out, into that subtle egoism which makes us pose either as victims or as martyrs.

In a very special manner this challenge is directed to contemporary Catholic youth. The very definition of their arrival in life includes a whole-hearted exuberance and freshness, a delight in service, a joy in being that brims full with creative promise. All of which is providential; for God intends that each new generation should be a kind of springtime for mankind, still another opportunity for effort that is redemptive and generous; once again a manifestation and a phase of the divine plan to eventually recreate, in a perpetual youthfulness, the cosmic totality in Christ.

This much is certain: by going enthusiastically unto the altar of God, bringing their sacrifices, their services unto him who alone is able to bring joy to their youth, our young people will disperse the shadows that presently envelop our century.

Otherwise, there will be night.

26 ✳ Christian Zeal

My food is to do the will of him who sent me, to accomplish his work. Do you not say, "There are yet four months, and then comes the harvest?" Well, I say to you, lift up your eyes and behold that the fields are already white for the harvest.

(Jn. 4:34–35)

A pure idea has not the strength to lift a straw off the ground.

Malebranche

As for us, we are philosophers not in word but in act; we do not say great things, but we do live them.

St. Cyprian

SHORTLY before his death the aged Pope Pius XI, with characteristic fired enthusiasm, commented that in our era "there is no place for mediocrity."

Tragically, its flabby, vapid presence is ubiquitous today. It is unquestionable that contemporary mankind offers countless heroes in the martyrdoms of blood-soaked pain and persistent dedication. But it seems that the majority of the human race —including us Christians whose very name spells heroism— are bent on becoming the "mob of unnecessary duplicates" that even Ahab (in Melville's *Moby Dick*) found wanting.

We recall Nietzsche's fiercely hysterical declaration that God is dead. Recently we have heard Sartre's Orestes shout to Jupiter, "I am neither master nor slave. I am my own freedom! Hardly hadst thou created me, when I already ceased to be thy own." Without the help of the Eternal, Camus assured us, we cannot create our own values. And the new dark nihilism would have us fight off qualms of conscience as we would flit away bothersome flies; for, so it claims, we must maintain the freedom to which we are condemned. Our earth-bound life, with its categories of accident, necessity, liberty, aloneness and senselessness, and its moral anarchy and pan-anxiety, is all that we have: death is a "door that shuts."

Of course, we would never consciously subscribe to this catechism of despair. We know that human life does have a providential pattern that opens to an eternity with God; and that we are ennobled to live in freedom in a perpetual challenge wherein we make moral choices, ultimately the definite choice between Christ and anti-Christ.

But it appears that this magnificent freedom is too weighty a burden for most of us. In practice we seem to agree with Fydor Dostoevsky's Grand Inquisitor: we prefer to sink into secure, comfortable lethargy than bear freedom. We want no real involvement in the disturbing pulsation of human, Christian existence. We deafen ourselves to the tumultuous cry of our brethren. If the sluice gates of evil be open, why bother us? With Tarrou in *The Plague*, we "leave it to others to make history." We merely wish to be provided with charming, titillating, Christian pleasantries, even grandiose ideas, and an occasional spiritual massage. Prophetic warnings (from the Popes and from the lonely "disturbers of humanity") fail to impress us: mankind will always have its wild, melancholy Cyclops hurling their devastations. We want no voices crying in our benign, benighted torpor.

To a very considerable degree the new mass media that increasingly blanket our existence contribute to the uprooting of our being from the full, vital dimensions of our Christian freedom, devitalizing our lives into spurious phantoms of what God wills them to be.

In "The Image Makers," William Lynch, S.J., focuses on preoccupation of the mass media with pseudo magnificences, arguing that they create illusions that gradually evaporate the dynamic out of our sensibility. With their banal dearth of the height and depth of genuine comedy and tragedy; their infallible, piddling vocabularies; their hymns to soaps, cigarettes and automobiles; their "personalities" (so often "talented" because they are celebrated, rather than celebrated because they are talented) who posture, with external smile and perfect pause, in the burning push of spotlights; with their fixities that root man's soul to the "big moment" rather than move from one insight to another—they provide an incredible, glittering masquerade that seduces our attention, shrinking the cosmos around us to petty, phony proportions—and us with it. Through systematized suggestion and exposure to subtle propaganda, and outright sensationalism, our minds and sensibilities become more and more vulnerable and submissive to manipulation by these media. As C. Wright Mills observes in *The Power Elite*, they "guide our very experience. Our standards of credulity, our standards of reality, tend to be set by these media rather than by our own fragmentary experience. Accordingly, even if the individual has direct, personal experience of events, it is not really direct and primary: it is organized in stereotypes. It takes long and skillful training to so uproot such stereotypes that an individual sees things freshly, in an unstereotyped manner." The superficialities of these media become "lenses" that strongly condition our acceptance or rejection of the things and ideals (including religious) and even persons that we come in contact in our daily living. Besides, it would be more correct to refer to the things and ideas and persons that these media allow us to communicate with, by reason of our culpable submissiveness to their direction. For, "the media tell the man in the mass who he is—they give him identity; they tell him what he wants to be—they give him aspirations; they tell him how to get that way—they give him technique; and they tell him how to feel that he is that way, even when he is not—they give him escape."

In sum, docile to manipulation by marketable mediocrity, progressively we are made just that: humanly shoddy, presenting "all the earmarks of insignificance." Like the characters in Ionesco's play, we capitulate and become malleable, and lose our full-dimensioned personalities—only that the outcome of our metamorphosis is far more appallingly barbaric than the grunting rhinoceros.

Often we defend our mediocrity by claiming that our goal is precisely Christian *peace*—the peace that Christ alone brings us (Jn. 14:27; Mk. 9:49; 2 Cor. 13:11). We want "peace with all men" (Rom. 12:17–18), the "peace of God, which surpasseth all understanding" (Phil. 4:7), nothing more nor less.

But we confuse peace and tranquility. Assuredly, "Peace is the tranquility of order," *pax est tranquillitas ordinis* (St. Thomas Aquinas), but the reverse is not true: peace is not order from tranquility. Peace is the fruit of love; love that gives itself, that moves to harmony, unity, as in God himself.

Like the character, Oblomov, in Goncharov's novel, we have "infinite dreams and infinite excuses." And our infinite dreams happen to be decadent, moribund caricatures of Christian life.

Our contemporary world, with its mounting challenges, is no place for paucity of soul; but, most assuredly, it has plenty of room for Christian zeal. This is the ardor of love of God that consumes and communicates (Abbot Marmion, O.S.B.); the transforming fire with which Christ, by his Spirit and through our being and action—its external manifestation—enkindles all creation (Lk. 12:49).

It is, in fact, the active participation in the holy intolerance of God with all infidelity to his Covenant. Significantly, the Greek word for zeal also means jealousy; and the English words, zeal and jealousy, both have the same Greek root. Our God is, indeed, "jealous in His love" (Ex. 20:4–5); his "very name speaks jealous love" (Ex. 54:14). Our God not only is love, he is *in* love—with us: we are truly his betrothed (2 Cor. 11:1–2). And our adulterous sin of infidelity (Ez. 16:14–16; 50:58) with "gods that are not gods" (De. 52:19–21) arouses the divine anger, which subsequently resorts to all the ingenious stratagems of love (Os. 2:6–8; De. 52:19, 21); and to punishments intended, not for the satisfaction of vengeance, but by way of evoking our remorse and return.

St. Paul, exemplary apostle, in his love for the Lord made his own the divine jealousy. He was jealous of God's house (Ps. 68:10)—the Church, "the stones that live and breathe" (1 Pt. 2:5)—with the consuming jealousy of God himself. In his epistles we witness his indefatigable concern for Christ's brethren, a solicitude that now and then flares into the same indignation already expressed, for instance, by Phinees in the Old Covenant (Nm. 25), and by our Lord himself in the New Covenant (Jn. 2:15–17). Christ's Church must be "a bride without stain" (2 Cor. 11:2) and must not be seduced and desecrated by the impious—within as well as outside the Church.

These, too, must be our sentiments.

Authentic Christian zeal is utterly selfish. It does not seek its own egotistic interests. It is not a maudlin, surreptitious winning of friends for oneself, but a constant self-effacing after the manner of the forerunner, whose sole desire was that Christ increase, he himself decrease (Jn. 3:22–30). For Christ is the Bridegroom of souls (2 Cor. 11:2): they belong to him. He is the Lord of all creation: the entire cosmos is his (Eph. 1:20–22). We are his coadjutors (1 Cor. 3:9), his ambassadors (2 Cor. 5:20), his friends (Jn. 15:15). Most decidedly we are not his competitors—an absurd role we sometimes strut in outrageous presumption.

This, of course, does not imply that this zeal is devoid of passion. Quite the contrary. It is personable, "strong as death" (Cant. 8:6). Like Paul, the true apostle knows how to abound in joy as well as to suffer (Phil. 4:12). His whole being rings resonantly with height and depth; his life is not the barren colorless counterfeit that so often parades as Christian. He realizes, with Grandmaison, that "the apostolate, to be fruitful, demands affective as well as effective gift of self." He loves his charges with a pure, expansive love that is splendidly Christ-like (Jn. 11:36; 13)—a love that, in its sincerity, does not hesitate to criticize constructively, despite the probability of ensuing loss of personal favor (2 Cor. 2:1–4).

Consequently, his zeal is without measure. It is no mere "renting out of services." It is boundless in its giving, even ready to forego apostolic joy (Phil. 1:23–25; 1 Thess. 2:7–8). Have we not received freely, in divine abandon, as it were? Then we too, in turn, must give freely (Mt. 10:8). The simple earnest words of the Apostle must be ours: "But I will most gladly spend myself and be spent to the limit for the sake of your souls, even though the more I love you, the less I am loved" (2 Cor. 12:15).

And it is alert, always endeavoring to anticipate the exigencies of the apostolate. "Lo, here am I, send me!" (Is. 6:8.) As the *Imitation of Christ* tells us, the apostle "flies, runs and rejoices; he is free and cannot be restrained."

Certainly, it is prudent; but prudent with the wisdom and the holy audacity that is given us by the Holy Spirit, and enlightened daring that meets with deep confidence the intimidations of evil (1 Cor. 10:13), not with the "prudence" of cowardice and opportunism.

While keenly earnest, Christian zeal remains patient. The true apostle is humble in the awareness of his own frailty. He, therefore, avoids the excess of imposing his own apostolic ideals and methods on his fellow-workers, as though HIS were the only ones worthwhile. He cooperates with them, "careful to keep the unity of the Spirit in the bond of peace" (Eph. 4:2–3)—otherwise his arrogance will provoke the envy and contention (Phil. 1:15–18) that rends the solidarity whereby Christ's Church is identifiable (Jn. 13:35). Moreover, the apostle reverences the sacred dignity of the individual human person. He realizes that "he who would be truly effective with men must respect *their* freedom, stir *their* initiatives, awaken *their* creative centers. Working with the impulses of living persons, he must freely accept all their false starts and detours" (Guardini). "Let him act with prudence," St. Benedict warns, "and not commit any excess, for fear that in being too eager to scrape the rust from the vessel and make it clean, he break it." For the Son of Man came not to destroy, but to save (Lk. 9:54–56; Mt. 12:20; Is. 42:3). Woe to the "apostle" who pushes people around!

Christian zeal shares in the plenitude of Christ's vision of reality (1 Cor. 2:16), one of universal proportions that embraces all creation. It recognizes all being, communes with all being, for all reflects the divine Truth and Goodness and Beauty, and all must be restored to God in Christ Jesus (Eph. 1:9–10). The true apostle shuns the shrunken, crabby worlds of prejudices and makes his own the ecumenical passion of Christ's Mystical Body for the total universe.

How different this Catholicism from the "bitter zeal" (St. Benedict) that flounders in the selfishness and hypocrisy of mediocrity!—the mediocrity that God bluntly damns as capable only of turning his stomach (Ap. 3:15–16).

27 * My Neighbor

As long as you did it to one of these, my least brethren, you did it to me.

(Mt. 25:40)

As regards our participation in beatitude, that is, in the life of Christ, there is a closer union between our soul and that of our neighbor than between our soul and body.

St. Thomas Aquinas

St. Francis deliberately did not see the wood for the trees. It is even more true that he deliberately did not see the mob for the men. . . . He only saw the image *of God multiplied but never monotonous. To him a man was always a man, and did not disappear in a dense crowd any more than in a desert. He honored all men . . . he not only loved but respected them all. . . . There was never a man who looked into those brown burning eyes without being certain that Francis Bernardone was really interested in him, in his own inner individual life from the cradle to the grave, that he himself was being valued and taken seriously. . . .*

G. K. Chesterton

Why do Catholics have such a harsh bite?

André Gide

In *The Diary of a Country Priest*, George Bernanos observed: "We are told that the earth is still quite young, after thousands of centuries still, as it were, in the pristine stages of its planetary evolution. *Evil, too, is only at its beginning*".

This forging ahead of evil that Bernanos perceived with tormented, prophetic insight is especially militant in the contemporary, unprecedented perversion of the very concept of man and of his destiny to love.

There is no denying the new awareness of individual human personality and of universal human solidarity in our era, nor the recent irrespressible spiritual upsurge of interdependence and communion between peoples, nor again the unparalleled heroism in the emancipation and betterment of the "masses." Mankind as a whole is growing in the knowledge, more or less formulated, of itself; and persons are confronting and (to a degree that makes the thinking Christian marvel) shouldering the challenge of actual, responsible brotherhood. In the vision of supernatural faith it is unmistakable that the torrent of energizing wisdom and love of the Holy Spirit is gradually, inexorably, penetrating and transforming the layers of refractory alienation that weigh down and splinter the human race.

But, in alarming juxtaposition to this outpouring of truth and benevolence, spumes a diabolical movement toward the annihilation of all that is genuine in man, individual and collective; a monstrous, formidable tide (Max Picard would attribute to it a structure) that advances across our globe, assaulting man, surreptitiously or by frontal attack depending on circumstances, and dispossessing him of the plenitude of his soul.

The sluice gates of hell are, indeed, thrown wide open! One may cite the infamous crimes committed against humanity perpetrated in our sanguinary epoch, crimes before whose heinousness and defilement the outrages of past centuries shrink. The beastial enormities of Nazi concentration camps —a Buchenwald, an Auschwitz—with their barbaric cruelties perfected by the latest insights into the human psyche, and their continuation under regimes such as the Communist; the putrefaction of an estimated eight million abortions performed annually in Japan alone; the modern ignominious defacement of death's mystery, "the dirty and horrible adventure," "A Dirty Trick;" the irresponsible manipulation of human sensibilities by the mass media that cut off man's creative receptivity to the inexhaustible, fertile richness of the cosmos, leaving him prostrate before Illusion; the foul, planned dissemination of hatred . . . the long, hybrid list is frightening. It would seem that many are obsessively bent on "proving" the grotesque definition of a human being in one of Sartre's novels: "a bit of thinking flesh that merely screams and bleeds when it is killed," nothing more; and on making our universe a loveless, chaotic waste under the reign of the Beast.

Flanked on all sides by such efforts to destroy God's image of truth and love in man, the Christian apostle—"christened" (Rom. 6:3) and receiving of the light of Christ's Resurrection—sees his fellowman in his integral being, as an individual person and as a member of the organic community, in the luminosity and perspectives of his faith. He knows that all created reality insofar as it reflects, even if inchoately, the Holiness who is God, is, in a profound sense, sacred; and that its presence should evoke from him an attitude essentially religious. But further, he deeply realizes that his daily encounter with man must be infinitely more reverent; for man bears such a concentration of being that, in relation to his Creator, his is truly the irreplaceable "image and glory of God" (1 Cor. 11:7). And more, infinitely more: the apostle remembers that God's Only-begotten has died for every human being (Rom. 14:15), thereby elevating each one to surpassing, inestimable value, even the most reprobate; and that this same charity continues, in momentous drama, to pursue and ennoble every man, working from within the innermost recesses of the person to elicit a return of love.

He knows existentially the many-faceted paradox of man: the embodied spirit, enveloped in conditions of time and space, who reaches into eternity; the "pride and refuse of the universe," whose grandeur can be inferred even from his wretchedness, as Pascal dared to write; the creature fallen and wounded by sin, who is redeemed in the sacrificial splendor of Christ; whose transcendent destiny is to be filled with all the fullness of God (Eph. 3:19), faithfully mirroring the essence of the divine Being (Mt. 5:48).

In other words, the Christian apostle confronts his neighbor, not as a mere "gelatinous job done in a dark room," and of no particular consequence, but as a creature of love, who has been redeemed by Love, and whose ultimate law of being is the return of love; who is rightly claimed by God alone, and whose profanation involves an incomparably odious, damning sacrilege.

Thus he honors and bears witness to man's delicate, strong sacredness, to the fierce and tender beauty of his being and of his vocation. Before all men—but with a special concern and sense of shared destiny, before those whom he serves in the apostolate—he is reverent with a deep religious wonder that remains young and fecund.

But this faith in which the apostle sees his neighbor must be informed by a vital principle (James 2:25–18) and this principle is supernatural love.

He is ever mindful that Christ has summoned him by a new commandment that he called his very own (Jn. 15:12); that "he who loves God also loves his brother" (1 Jn. 4:21); and that the whole law of Christian liberty (without which freedom supernatural love is impossible) is fulfilled in this one, royal precept (Gal. 5:14; Ja. 2:8), the love of neighbor.

And let the perennial question be asked again: Who is my neighbor? "You are one, and your neighbors are many," advised St. Augustine. "Mark well, in fact, that your neighbor is not only your brother, your relative, your ally. Every man has all men for his neighbors. We feel father and son to be close, father-in-law and son-in-law. *But there is nothing so close to a man as another man.*" The apostle's neighbor is the ingrate, the intellectual, the saintly, the blue-eyed, the outcast, the poor, the hypocrite, the innocent, the wealthy, the capricious, the dark-skinned, the brutish, the charming, the idiot, the innocent, the alcoholic . . . *homo quidam,* to whom he is indebted (Rom. 1:14), and who augments him; each and every human being, in all that person's uniqueness, in all the unremitting, splendid, tortured, flexible reality of everyday existence.

United to Christ the apostle receives of the Holy Spirit a created participation in the very love of God himself (1 Jn. 4:7; Gal. 5:22), whereby he is enabled to love as God loves; and the same love that he raises to God, he also opens to his neighbor. Love of God is, indeed, impossible without charity to one's fellowman; to claim otherwise is to lie (1 Jn. 4:20). As a matter of fact, love of God presses the apostle with a holy violence into the dedicated service of others (2 Cor. 5:14).

But this is no mere philanthrophy terminating in man, noble and worthy though it be. Its movement and ultimate goals are not limited to this life, but, in accordance with man's transcendent quality, expand and burst into the eternal. Its orientation is not to man simply as man, but to man—even the least of human society—mysteriously identified with Christ (Mt. 25:34–35), perhaps one of the members of his Mystical Body, "of his flesh and of his bones" (Eph. 5:29–30). It is with God and in God and for God that the apostle loves his neighbor. And he loves him, not only in service that is directly oriented to his neighbor's eternal salvation (his primary concern), but, as far as he is able, and with a calm that is ever conscious of Divine Providence, in service that is concerned with his neighbor's temporal welfare—as Christ himself did (Acts 10:38). For man's eternal destiny is rooted in and shaped by the here-and-now, bewilderingly complex details of his temporal existence; and besides, temporal good is, in itself, pleasing to the Almighty (Gn. 1).

Manichaean damnings aside, clearly it is no counterfeit, no vague religiosity, a surface of words, a series of empty demonstrations that wallow in mawkish sentiment and that soon deflate; but rather a vigorous, efficacious proof of love by the sure test of authentic action (1 Jn. 3:17–18), blazing fire that recreates all that it touches.

It is *agape* not *eros:* without measure (Lk. 6:38); never self-seeking (1 Cor. 13:4–7) but utterly considerate of others (Phil. 2:4); audaciously prepared to offer total sacrifice in the wine-press of martyrdom, in imitation of Christ, Redeemer.

Nor is it "cold sacrifice untouched by tenderness," a meager, tight-clenched forbearance; not a matter of calculated, impersonal business (after the manner of some "charity" offices); never patronizing, a doubtful courtesy; but it is patient, kind —with the kindness of God (Ti. 3:4) who is moved by the cry of suffering from within man's heart—unpretentious, accessible, sympathetic, welcoming, joyous (1 Cor. 8:4–7; Col. 3:12–13).

It would be possible to enlarge on the concept of charity without ever coming to a halt, for its dimensions are infinite as God. But here we content ourselves with one more characteristic of this supernatural love in its actual operation in our space-time context. *It demands direct, reciprocal, human encounter.*

It is of capital importance that this truth be appreciated, for impersonal service to others, massively organized through modern media, is increasingly paraded as authentic Christian charity. Granted that supernatural love of one's neighbor may well, and often necessarily, use many of the modern organizational methods of communication and service; they may never supplant the immediate, personal approach. Just as the divine Word, eternally pronounced by absolute love, was made flesh in order that love be efficaciously, redeemingly expressed, so must the love of the apostle for his neighbor be incarnated in the sacramental flesh of his own corporality—and not merely in books, food, clothing, advertisements: *things.*

Writes E. Schillebeeckx: "The Son of God really did become Man—become, that is to say, a human spirit which, through its own proper bodiliness, dwelt visibly in our world. The incarnation of the divine life, therefore, involves bodily aspects. Together with this, we must remember that every human exchange, or the intercourse of men one with another, proceeds in and through man's bodiliness. When a man exerts spiritual influence on another, encounters through the body are necessarily involved. The inward man manifests itself as a reality that is in this world through the body. It is in his body, and through his body, that man is open to the 'outside,' and that he makes himself present to his fellow men. Human encounter proceeds through the visible obviousness of the body, which is a sign that reveals and at the same time veils the human interiority."

Consequently, authentic love of one's neighbor, in its full amplitude, must be extended through personal, direct action and word—especially the true, potent word, spoken to another, springing from the depths of the human spirit, being a manifestation of one's intimate being; a revelation, by reciprocal interpenetration of consciences, of one's personal mystery, and therefore of love.

These truths were confirmed and consecrated by Christ himself, our model in the apostolate. He went directly to people, he was available to their direct approach, he conversed with them. He was not content with distant, interior inspiration of their being, nor with up-to-the-minute bulletins, nor longer even with great prophets. He *encountered*, in a fully human, personal, direct manner, his brethren whom he had come to redeem, in the myriad ramifications of their existence.

To realize such encounter the Word crossed the infinite. In order that the apostle may faithfully continue his mission of love, he asks that he cross a street, a city, or only a continent.

By thus practicing the truth in love, we, who are the Church, grow in Christ, our Head; and so the Mystical Body builds itself up in love (Eph. 4:15–16). "Every day the Church brings forth the Church!" (St. Bede the Venerable)

28 ✱ God's Glory

Give thanks to the Lord, invoke his Name; make known among the nations his deeds. . . . Glory in his Name; rejoice, O hearts that seek the Lord! Look to the Lord in his strength; seek to serve him constantly: recall the wondrous deeds that he was wrought, his portents and the judgments he has uttered.

(Ps. 104:1–5)

I honor my Father . . . I do not seek my own glory . . ."

(Jn. 8:49–50)

My soul magnifies the Lord!

(Lk. 1:46)

THROUGHOUT his lifetime on earth, Jesus had one consuming desire to which he referred all his activity—the glory of the divinity (Jn. 8:49–55). It was his inexhaustible love for his Father that motivated his entire apostolate, that impelled him to bring back an alienated mankind to the exaltation of God, and that finally "drained" him of divine prerogatives in crucified abandonment.

Jesus Christ was no mere "man for others," as some liberal Protestants insist. His total being, throughout its ontological recesses, was shot through with the consuming desire to glorify his Father (Jn. 8:49–55), the love who gives (Rom. 5:5–6); and in pursuit of this glorification Christ continued the movement of *agape* that begins eternally in the Father, extending it to the "others," his brethren.

The glorified Christ continues his mission of praise. Now lifted above the cosmos (Jn. 12:32), he draws to himself the prodigious two-fold movement of glorification within the works of Creation and Redemption, gathering all in himself in one immeasurable act of homage. Through his Mystical Body he envelops he whole breadth of created being, its intense pulsing structure and its straining towards fulfillment, in a love that vivifies and consecrates.

One with the Church, we identify ourselves with this vast tide of glorification that moves through Christ to God. Should we cooperate with the graces offered us by the Holy Spirit, we too, like a John the Baptist, a Francis Xavier, or a Therese Martin, are smitten by the "ailment" of God's infinite splendor, the unique torment that seizes and absorbs the total human personality, urging the apostle to seek passionately the heights of God's external glory. For in the dark luminosity of faith we contemplate the divine glory of Christ (Jn. 1:14), an experience that necessarily brims over into the exacting engagements of the apostolate.

Here again we perceive the inter-relationship between the Eucharistic Sacrifice and the Church's apostolate. It is in the Mass that the two currents of creation and redemption merge and are transformed in Christ's supreme act of worship, the highest expression of creation's glorification of God. And Christ, in vital communion with his Mystical Body in the sacred mystery is God's acceptance of creation's outburst of praise. Consequently, our apostolate may be considered the bringing of mankind (and through mankind the teeming universe) to insertion in the Eucharistic action, and thereby to participation in Christ's glorification of the divinity.

Such are the magnificent perspectives of apostolic aspirations!

But, notwithstanding good faith and zeal, our activity is shot through with temptations; and, unless we be docile to the guidance of Christ's Spirit, the outcome of these activities will be disastrous.

For instance, there is always the subtle human tendency to steal for oneself some of the glory that belongs only to God. We protest with horror at the very idea of this diabolical perversion; but the inclination to identify God's cause with our own partialities and prejudices lurks within our weakness, ready to ambush our purity of intention. We would make his Church our own private property, or even shrink it, moribund, within the confines of our own diocese, our own parish, our own congregation, our own organization; and we would reduce the apostolate to an insidious inflation of our own ego.

Or, again, impatient with the apparently slow workings of divine grace, we become insatiably eager for immediate, tangible results to our efforts—efforts that are now, as a matter of fact, rendered impotent by lack of communion with Christ. We would seek the advance of God's glory by dubious means, deluding ourselves into believing that such is possible by mere human salesmanship.

We are even tempted to distort the very meaning of God's glory. Forgetting the truth that it is essentially by identification with the glorifying power of our Lord's Passion that the apostle bears witness to the divinity, we grow disconcerted by the paradox of the Cross and recoil with revulsion from its ever-pressing reality. Christ assuredly wishes us to mobilize the resplendence of creation to the service of his Spouse; but the Holy Spirit reminds us that the Church's essential glory lies hidden (Eph. 5:23–33)—deep in the adherence of his members to the divine will and in their sharing in his life. All this does not satisfy us. We must have dazzling triumph, not the reproach of the Cross. And our itch for the accumulation of success and prestige around Christ's Church ultimately leads to the impasse of calculated compromise with the world.

It would be downright folly to minimize the danger inherent in these temptations. But, at the same time, we must remember that, upheld by the power of the divine Son, and motivated by the exigencies of a selfless love, we too can contribute our humble share to the glorification of the One who is All-Holy.

29 ✳ The Temporal Order

And he, trembling and amazed, said: "Lord, what wilt thou have me do?" And the Lord said to him: "Arise, and go into the city . . ."

(Acts 9:6)

Christianity is not an obstacle to modern progress, because it does not consider modern progress only in its technical and economic aspects, but in its total development. Temporal goods can certainly help the full development of man, but they do not constitute the ideal of human perfection nor the essence of social progress.

The Christian sees in temporal goods the work and the gifts of God. As such he admires them and puts them to his use, but they do not become his idol. He always remembers the first commandment: "Thou

shalt have no other God but me." It is there that the
drama of the confrontation between the Christian and
the temporal order is born.

Pope Paul VI

We are charged to bring the future to birth!

Charles Péguy

CHRIST ADDRESSES the twentieth century lay apostle with
the same words with which he directed Paul: "Arise, go into
the city!"—the City of Man. The great world of human civilization must make progress, and, speaking, it absolutely cannot
advance to its full, true destiny apart from the Christian's
commitment. He must be present like leaven within the City
of Man: guided by the Holy Spirit—whose power quickened
the beginnings of the cosmos—and geared to efficient action
he must lead it to its total development.

It would seem hardly necessary to insist that the Christian
has a mission to accomplish other than the apostolate as such;
that is, the human effort, attainable by man's natural abilities,
that terminates in the humanizing transformation of the
material and spiritual riches latent in the universe of man and
things. For as man, the paragon of creatures in this myriad existence, he is committed (Gn. 1:22) to a prodigious, cosmic
mission of collaboration with the Almighty in the painful
labor of Creation—a task distinct but inseparable, in the unity
of the Christian's personality, from his involvement in the
economy of redemption.

But there are critics in plenty who accuse Christians with
neglect of the temporal order. This "pie in the sky" indict-
ment is often hurled with overt contempt by men blind to
abundant evidence by reason of their hatred for Christ. However, the complaint also comes from persons of unimpeachable

sincerity. For there are far too many Catholics who remain satisfied in the stupor of complacency and sloth, content with leaving to others the unremitting toil necessary in the building of the City of Man. There are those as well who believe in a false transcendence, whose outlook on reality is distorted by a kind of religious neurosis, a sterile acosmic piety that rejects the tangible wonders of creation and scorns man's civilizing attempts.

The authentic lay Christian (as opposed to the mediocre and the caricature) is aware that "we must love God through creation, and creation through God," that enrichment of our piety towards the world is inseparable from an advance in our piety towards God. He agrees with Nietzsche that the "Universe is deep," but he knows that these finite depths strain beyond themselves to the mysteries of the divinity, that they are fully of a mysterious expectancy (Rom. 8:19); for he learns the subtle transparencies in creation, its sacramental structure. At the same time he confronts its enigma, its opaqueness, the dark wound that reflects the terrifying rupture inflicted within his own being by man's first transgression against God. And he experiences the inescapable need for purification in his relationship with creation, the constant demand for humble detachment and renunciation, without which creation can become a vertigo that lures to idolatry and slavery.

The authentic lay Christian is alert to the duties involved in his communion with creation: the prodigious enterprise of organization by which (as farmer, scientist, engineer, laborer, as *homo faber*) he fulfills it from without; and his profound work of contemplation (as artist and philosopher) whereby he strives, as Jean Mouroux wrote, to express its very essence from within. As man—whether he be fisherman, potter, poet, nurse, physicist—he is creation's priest. But more: he is Christian, he is a man renewed in Christ, a member of a new priesthood; his special lay vocation is to encompass, purify and elevate the "mighty Octave of Creation" (Paul Claudel) in a redeeming, consecrating love that delivers it from the "servitude of corruption" (Rom. 8:19–23). Already he is, in the glorified *Kyrios*, part of a redeemed and transfigured humanity; he is a living member of the Mystical Body of Christ whose divine, vital impetus reaches out to man and all creation, purifying, assimilating, integrating, transforming all being to its deepest fibers, so that from within the old, sun-shadowed world, that gradually passes away (1 Cor. 7:31), a new, interiorized totality be formed—a new mankind, a new heaven, a new earth (Eph. 4:24; Ap. 21:1).

These considerations indicate—inadequately, for the dignity and the responsibility involved are of ineffable splendor—the lay apostle's destiny as co-creator and co-redeemer (both terms, of course, used analogously) with the Word, by the power of the Holy Spirit. They are complementary; both missions must be accomplished before Christ's Second Coming. In other words, *the cosmic mission of the Christian, his gigantic task in the temporal order, contains an urgency.* Man, by reason of his God-given nature, needs its progressive fulfillment in his movement towards the Trinity; indeed, by divine dispensation, it is required by Christ himself in the building up of his Mystical Body, a truth, of far-reaching implications that is not sufficiently recognized.

But the authentic Christian does not endorse the hoax advocated by Communists and the like: the blasphemous and futile myth of a paradise on earth constructed by humanity itself, a salvation of man by man. Certainly he will do his utmost to further mankind's cultural progress; but always he is aware of the ever present evils of sin and death. He never forgets that, apart from Christ, man is not integrally human, let alone divinized. He is aware that the whole cosmos cannot possibly attain its fulfillment of itself while cultural achievements must be striven for, although they are real values in themselves (their splendor eternally recognized and blessed in the glorified Humanity of the Incarnate Word) they contribute nothing to the true liberation and rehabilitation of humanity unless they are guided by the Spirit of God.

He is also humbly aware that his mission to dominate and shape creation is fraught with chilling responsibilities, that it is in itself a perilous test of his human caliber. He knows that unless he rise to the measure of full responsibility—to the cosmos, to his fellowman, to himself, to his God—the power at his disposal will lead to global catastrophe and the corruption and dissolution of all that is human in his own being. He nurses no illusions regarding mankind's present condition: he carries within himself the disquieting realization that contemporary man's wielding of power over nature has far outstripped his responsible control of his own person. The challenge confronting him is all the more urgent.

Nor does he delude himself with facile rationalization into thinking that he has in his possession the one solution—*the* Christian solution—for the detailed, complex, cultural, poltical and economic problems confronting contemporary mankind. He realizes the pressing significance of Karl Rahner's shrewd observation: that "Christians *as such* simply do not have any ready-made concrete program for the conduct of the state, or of culture, or of economics, and that in fact *cannot* have one. This was indeed theoretically the case in earlier ages. . . . It did not appear so plainly because the area of possibilities historically available for human realization was relatively narrow. It is now going to become gradually clear that the gap between universal Christian principles and the putting of them in practice in any one of a number of possible forms is a gap as wide as the possibilities now opening up before us. From this it follows that we Christians should indeed rejoice that it is given to us to have the true standards by which human living can be shaped according to its meaning . . . yet we cannot as *Christians* have any single, unitary program, when it comes to planning in the concrete."

The Christian apostle avoids the dangerous error of those extremists who, infatuated by one aspect of truth to the neglect of its totality, embrace what Father William Lynch terms "the mentality of the clear idea . . . that spares itself the effort of thought that is involved in relating itself to other ideas." These are the "accredited trustees" of authentic Christianity for whom there is never an inter-penetrating of realities, but always mutual, intense attack. Theirs is the limbo (decidedly not the Christian world) crammed with polarities that prescind from the basic opposition between normal right and wrong—warring labels that generate divisiveness, passions and bitter partisanship.

The true Christian cooperates with others in the building of the City—and not only with his Christian brethren, but with all his fellowmen. In a world that is no longer the Christendom of the West, where the Church could stamp its ideals on public life, he knows that innumerable institutions—cultural, political, economic, local, national and international—have evolved, and are continuing to evolve, whose origins have no immediate influence whatsoever from the Church. He is aware that many of these institutions are excellent: he is certainly not one who subscribes to the heretical notion that anything outside the control of the Church is thereby condemned as something evil in its constitution. He cooperates with his contemporary non-Christian neighbors in all that is truly human.

The difficulties and evils that attend the present turning-point in history and the obstacles to religion that accompany our contemporary technological civilization do not destroy his hope for man's future; for his hope is not founded on mere technique, but on Christ, the Alpha and the Omega of all creation. As Rahner comments, in his usual forthright manner: "In the Incarnation and the Cross, God has made a total and final decision (without prejudice to human freedom) in favor of the world and the natural order as saved, glorified, and to be given beatitude through the victory of grace. The drama is no longer in the balance; world history is already, in principle, decided; and the decision is for its salvation." This is the optimism that grounded on the Incarnation of the Word, an optimism that persists even on the Cross.

The lay apostle lives by the rhythm of the Church's existence, that of the Paschal mystery, and applies himself zealously to the cosmic mission in the conviction that he will not be less Christian by being more a man. Is not his Exemplar the One who, in divine earnestness, became man irrevocably; who became human more than we; and whose glorified humanity still retains the stamp of the carpenter's trade that he pursued in the temporal order?